**TO MY LATE BROTHER,
BILL BONNSTETTER:**

Within these pages lies not just the culmination of our shared journey in exploring the five sciences of self but also a testament to your visionary leadership at TTI Success Insights. Though you are no longer with us, your unwavering commitment to unraveling the complexities of human potential has been the guiding light for our endeavors. This book, rooted in the principles that you championed, is a tribute to your enduring legacy in the world of self-assessments.

Your foresight and passion have not only shaped TTI Success Insights into a beacon of excellence but also inspired countless individuals to unlock their true selves. As we present these insights, each word resonates with the wisdom and dedication you exemplified throughout your remarkable life's work.

With enduring love and profound respect,

Dr. Ronald Bonnstetter

This book is also dedicated to every individual whose life has been profoundly transformed by the personal assessments pioneered by Bill Bonnstetter, whose spirit and vision continue to inspire the journey of self-discovery at TTI Success Insights. This book stands as a testament to the transformative power of understanding oneself, bridging the gap between Bill's legacy and the personal growth stories that have emerged from his innovations, including my own.

Bill Bonnstetter's work at TTI Success Insights was not just about creating a company; it was about fostering a community where the exploration of human potential could thrive. His dedication to the five sciences of self has equipped us with the tools necessary for introspection and growth.

In honoring the legacy of Bill and the life-changing experiences of those touched by his work, this book aims to light the way for future explorations of self-understanding and personal achievement.

With heartfelt appreciation and respect,

Carissa Gwerder Collazo, MS

CONTENTS

Introduction	7
1 Harnessing People's Potential, Now and in the Future	17
2 The Science of DISC	33
3 The Science of Motivation	53
4 The Science of Workplace Competencies	77
5 The Science of Emotional Intelligence	97
6 The Science of the Hartman Value Profile	119
Conclusion: Sciences of Self in Business Today and Tomorrow	145
Connect	153
Acknowledgments	155
About the Authors	157
Index	161

INTRODUCTION

In the intricate world of human interaction and personal growth, there lies a spectrum of social sciences dedicated to unraveling the interwoven web of what drives us, how we act, and why we make the decisions we do. This book offers an expansive exploration of five key disciplines—DISC, motivation, workplace competencies, emotional intelligence, and the Hartman Value Profile—that have woven their narratives through the history of psychological and sociological thought. These disciplines, each with their own rich histories, are the quintessential tools used by TTI Success Insights (TTI) to craft assessments that are as informative as they are transformative.

- **DISC**, the behavioral assessment framework based on the pioneering work of William Moulton Marston and Prescott Lecky, dissects behaviors into four primary traits, clarifying how individuals interact with others and their surroundings. It has been refined over decades to become a leading tool in understanding workplace dynamics and personal engagement strategies.

- The study of **motivation,** influenced by the ancient theories of Aristotle, Plato, and Socrates, delves into the very essence of what propels us forward, what inspires us to rise each day and strive for more. The pursuit to comprehend these drivers has given birth to motivational models that are crucial in personal development and organizational leadership.

- **Workplace competencies** capture the essence of what makes an individual not just adequate but exceptional in their role. This branch of study looks beyond academic qualifications and technical skills to identify the inherent attributes that contribute to an individual's effectiveness within their professional sphere.

- **Emotional intelligence**, a relatively modern addition championed by Daniel Goleman, Ph.D., and based on the work of John D. Mayer and Peter Salovey, has revolutionized how we think about success and leadership. It emphasizes the essential roles of self-awareness, self-regulation, empathy, and social skills in achieving personal and professional success.

- Finally, the **Hartman Value Profile**, rooted in Robert S. Hartman's formal axiology, provides a unique approach to understanding judgment and decision-making. It evaluates the intrinsic, extrinsic, and systemic value individuals assign to different aspects of their lives, offering profound insights into their moral and ethical compasses.

TTI Success Insights harnesses the power of these five social sciences to create assessments that reflect an individual's capabilities and pave the way for growth and improvement. Through a synergy of these disciplines, TTI's assessments provide a multi-dimensional analysis of individuals, empowering them to realize their potential in both personal and professional realms.

THE DRIVING QUESTION

In our work with brain imaging, we delve into the intricate processes of decision-making as an individual responds to self-reporting assessments. In essence, we are deeply interested in what drives people to answer the assessment questions the way they do. We work to uncover the neural pathways that illuminate how individuals perceive themselves and their capabilities. Our dedication to this research is fueled by the belief that understanding the cognitive mechanisms behind self-evaluation can significantly enhance the precision of our tools.

Our focus is on revealing the subconscious dynamics that shape responses during self-assessment. This understanding is vital for developing assessments that are not only reflective of an individual's true self but can also offer predictive insights into their potential. The significance of this research is rooted in its potential impact on personal and organizational development. Correlating the underlying neurological pathways of human decision-making with these assessments is impacting both our understanding as well as assessment accuracy. Our work with brain imaging is a step toward a future where self-assessments can be verified with actual cognitive and emotional states, thus offering a more authentic snapshot of an individual's abilities and potential.

THE IMPORTANCE OF UNDERSTANDING YOURSELF

Understanding personal attributes in business is not a mere luxury; it is an essential element in fostering healthy, productive, and harmonious work environments. It is the golden key that unlocks the potential within individuals and teams, and it drives innovation, collaboration, and organizational success.

The importance of comprehending human behavior transcends professional development; it is the bedrock upon which meaningful relationships are built, conflicts are resolved, and inclusive environments are cultivated.

Understanding your own personal attributes and those of your friends, family, and colleagues has long-term and far-reaching positive results. It completely changed my (Ronald's) teaching style in the early years of my career and steered my career trajectory later in life.

I loved teaching. Over my 40-year teaching career, I have taught 8th grade, high school, and junior college, as well as 29 years in a university setting. During this time, I received a number of honors, including serving as editor of an international journal and several national teaching awards. The most interesting part, though, is that I started out as a truly terrible teacher.

In my first year of teaching, I entered the classroom with a plan, dreaming of how my students would walk out of my class nine months later with knowledge and excitement about sharing the secondary science curriculum. But for all my preparation, I was missing a crucial piece of the teaching puzzle: a deep understanding of my own personal attributes and those of my students. Unaware of the differences in learning, behavior, motivation, and communication among adults and students alike, I taught, communicated, and tested according to what made sense to me—my own style.

> **I didn't understand that my own style might not be the best way to teach every student.**

This lack of self-awareness often led to miscommunications and misunderstandings with my students and colleagues. Without recognizing the diverse styles of my students, I struggled to work with their varied learning styles and motivational triggers. My lessons,

INTRODUCTION

though meticulously planned, failed to engage my students, and the once-excited faces quickly turned bored, frustrated, or indifferent.

My inability to understand where my students were coming from, both in terms of their personal backgrounds and their personal motivators, created a divide in the classroom. The disconnect was palpable.

It wasn't until a family get-together that first Thanksgiving fall break that I got my first tool to teach more effectively. After dinner, I was talking to my brother, Bill, about how my year was going. Being 12 years older than me, he had a little more experience in life and career, so I pretended to listen to him—even though he didn't have a Ph.D.

I patiently listened to his discoveries and successes in personal attributes assessments over the years, ready to roll my eyes internally. But right in the middle of my skepticism, he caught my attention.

"Ron, you have a classroom full of students who communicate, learn, understand, and react in unique ways. Furthermore, you need to understand that your preferred style may differ wildly from that of your students. What are you doing to reach each and every one of them?"

Well, that stopped me in my Ph.D., know-it-all tracks. My students all learn and communicate differently from me? Little bells and lights started going off in my head as I thought about some of the issues I had been having with them.

Some of my students would stop by my office after class, seeking clarity on a particular topic. Valuing efficiency, I would give them a rapid-fire explanation. With looks of confusion, they would respond with questions to get a more thorough understanding but eventually give up on my abrupt responses. The students would leave the meeting looking more confused, commenting to each other that I didn't have the time or patience for their questions while I was perplexed, believing I had given a clear and concise explanation.

I also thought about some students who had meticulously presented their research during their presentations, ensuring every detail was backed by thorough data, while I liked to focus on big-picture outcomes and quick decision-making. After their presentations, I would point out broader aspects they could improve upon, emphasizing the need to be more concise and get to the main points faster for the sake of audience engagement.

These students valued accuracy and precision and felt deflated. They had spent countless hours checking every fact and including every detail to avoid potential errors. They hoped I would recognize their dedication to thoroughness. Instead, I overlooked their efforts in favor of brevity, and they felt that I didn't appreciate the depth and rigor of their work, while I was left wondering why they focused so much on minute details at the expense of a more engaging delivery.

Humbling myself, I asked Bill for advice. He graciously offered the DISC assessment, a model for assessing behavioral styles, to me and my students for free. Not having any other idea or insight, I decided to give it a go. I integrated it into my coursework to help my students understand themselves better.

In the process of assessing myself, I realized that I didn't know myself any better than my students knew themselves. I finally understood that *I* was the problem, not my students. I even created a chart, which allowed me to see that the majority of my students were spread across five to ten o'clock on the Style Insights DISC wheel, and I was over at two o'clock. The entire behavioral styles of the class and my natural style were a total mismatch.

INTRODUCTION

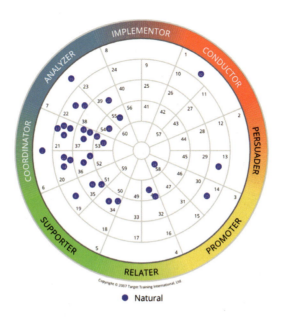

This diagram shows data from students in one of my University of Nebraska Science Methods class. My behavioral style is represented by the blue dot in cell number 1.

The more I learned, the more I adjusted and changed my teaching, responses, and testing style. By understanding myself and my students better, I was able to bridge the gap and create a more harmonious, effective learning environment.

My second year as a professor was a complete turnaround from the first year. I even wrote a story about my student assessment integration and the change that occurred, which won a national award for outstanding teacher preparation.

As I got ready to receive the award, Carl Sagan, the presenter, told me, "I have no idea why I'm giving you this award. Give me your elevator pitch."

I quickly replied, "I teach the science of self."

NATURAL SCIENCE VERSUS SOCIAL SCIENCE

Mankind has always sought wisdom, defined by some as "applied knowledge." Another way of describing wisdom may be "good judgment." Judgment is the ability to understand an issue, the context, and constraints, and consider all factors to come to the best possible opinion or decision about a matter.

Judgment (evaluation and decision-making) is an integral part of the social sciences. It is necessary for psychology, sociology, anthropology, economics, political science, management, law, and linguistics. In contrast to the natural sciences, the social sciences have been built on philosophy, the study of knowledge collected and debated over thousands of years.

Over the last four centuries, advances in modern science, driven by the evolution of pure mathematics, have led to significant discoveries and improvements in various aspects of human life. While not all applications of science have been beneficial, the overall impact has been profound.

In contrast, the social sciences have struggled to keep pace due to the absence of a comparable formal and evolving logical framework. This has resulted in a lesser degree of certainty and consistency in social science theories and practices compared to natural sciences. The disparity is evident in educational curricula, where social sciences are less emphasized, and experts often find themselves in disagreement over various principles and theories.

If any of the great philosophers or moral leaders 2,000 years ago were to visit our planet today, they would be amazed at the technological and scientific advances we have made as human beings. At the same time, they would probably be equally surprised by the lack of progress made in the social sciences over the past 2,000 years.

INTRODUCTION

The future of human development lies in the merging of these two worldviews. The natural sciences could greatly benefit from an expanded view of reality that incorporates philosophical possibilities, and social science fields such as psychology need to embrace the latest advancements in neurology. TTI's assessments are developed with this merging at the core.

WHAT DO ASSESSMENTS DO?

Assessments act as a lens, bringing into focus the subtle, often unarticulated aspects of our personalities. They translate our internal nuances into tangible insights, providing a language to describe what we innately feel but struggle to express. This process of reflection and categorization helps uncover hidden strengths and areas for improvement, enhancing self-awareness. By articulating these internal characteristics, assessments enable a deeper understanding of ourselves, facilitating better communication and decision-making in various aspects of life.

> **In addition to personal introspection, assessments are key in fostering an understanding of others.**

Assessments reveal the diversity in human thought and behavior, promoting empathy and effective communication. This is especially beneficial in collaborative settings, where adapting to different perspectives is crucial. Assessments act as bridges, connecting diverse viewpoints and aiding in creating harmonious and productive relationships in both personal and professional environments.

Lastly and perhaps most importantly, assessments highlight the importance of diversity by showcasing the richness that different personalities and perspectives bring. They challenge the notion of homogeneity, showing that a mix of traits leads to more creative and effective outcomes. Assessments emphasize the value of diversity in teams and communities, demonstrating that a range of ideas and approaches is essential for innovation and success in a complex, multifaceted world.

As we delve into the origin of DISC, motivation, workplace competencies, emotional intelligence, and the Hartman Value Profile, we have the capacity to begin a transformative journey that goes beyond the conventional boundaries of personal and professional development. These disciplines, explored within the pages of this book, are not mere academic concepts but vibrant, dynamic forces that shape the essence of our interactions, motivations, and aspirations. They offer a lens through which we can view ourselves and the world around us with greater clarity, empathy, and understanding. This exploration is not just about assessing where we stand; it's about unlocking the vast potential that lies within each of us, waiting to be harnessed.

In this context, the work of TTI Success Insights guides us through the intricate landscape of human behavior and cognitive processes. By integrating cutting-edge brain imaging research with the foundational principles of these five social sciences, we are offered a unique opportunity to bridge the gap between self-perception and reality. This synergy between neuroscience and social science paves the way for assessments that reflect our true selves and are instrumental in charting a course for growth, improvement, and ultimately, personal and professional success. This book is an invitation to embark on that journey, to explore the depths of our own potential, and to navigate the future with confidence, insight, and purpose.

HARNESSING PEOPLE'S POTENTIAL, NOW AND IN THE FUTURE

I'll never forget the adventure that began on a crisp, sunny morning with my brother Bill. We were embarking on a unique project, one that combined his love for the countryside and his keen interest in human behavior. Bill had this intriguing idea: he believed that by observing farmsteads, he could correlate their observable characteristics with the behavior styles of their owners and thus design more effective sales strategies. As a middle schooler who was killing time hanging with my adult brother, I was skeptical at first, but as we set out in his old pickup truck, my curiosity was piqued.

Our first stop was a farm that I'd passed many times but never really noticed. As we drove up the lane, Bill pointed out a shiny new John Deere tractor parked prominently in front. Yet, the rest of the farm was in disarray. Tools were strewn about, and the barn looked like it needed repairs. Bill chuckled and said, "See that? This farmer is driven, ambitious, but not too concerned with details or order." I was amazed at how he could glean so much from just a glance.

As we continued our journey from one farm to another, Bill's observations grew more fascinating. I remember one farm in particular that struck me. It was different from the rest. Hollyhocks lined the driveway, leading up to a charming house surrounded by a white picket fence. Everything was in perfect order. The lawn was manicured, and even the garden tools were neatly arranged. Bill's eyes lit up as he observed, "This is meticulousness at its finest. This farmer is detail-oriented, organized, and cautious. Selling to them will need precision, answering every question, and ensuring we meet their needs."

Every farm told a different story, and Bill interpreted each one with such enthusiasm and accuracy. His approach varied with each observation. At one farm, he planned an energetic sales pitch, knowing the farmer would appreciate boldness and efficiency. At another, he prepared for a detailed presentation, understanding the farmer's need for thoroughness and precision.

Those weekends with Bill were more than just drives through the countryside; they were lessons in understanding people beyond the surface. Bill's method, though unconventional, was brilliant. He taught me to look beyond the obvious, to see the subtle cues in people's environments that reflected their personalities and behavior styles.

> **That experience shaped my approach to understanding human behavior.**

It was more than just a project; it was a journey into the depths of personality and a testament to Bill's innovative spirit and his extraordinary ability to read people. His insights on those drives laid the groundwork for what would become a groundbreaking approach to behavioral assessment. As for me, I walked away with not just memories of those scenic drives, but also a newfound appreciation for the complexity and diversity of human behavior and just how much can be gleaned by focused observation.

TTI SUCCESS INSIGHTS' CUTTING-EDGE ASSESSMENTS

Over 40 years later, under Bill's enduring vision and passion, TTI Success Insights is driven by a primary mission to unlock human potential through our cutting-edge Science of Self™ assessments. This commitment is not just about creating effective tools for today; it encompasses a relentless pursuit of research, innovation, and enhancement in our products and processes.

Central to TTI's ethos is a dedication to ongoing scientific validation. This means our assessments are not static; they are continuously scrutinized and refined based on the latest research in psychology, behavioral science, and data analysis. Such validation ensures the tools remain accurate, reliable, and relevant to modern workplace challenges and dynamics.

Moreover, new product development is a cornerstone of TTI's approach. The workforce and workplace are in constant states of evolution, influenced by technological advancements, changing societal values, and global trends. In response, we are committed to developing new products that meet these changing needs, helping organizations and individuals adapt and thrive in a dynamic work environment. This includes creating new assessments that accurately measure emerging competencies and skills required in the future workforce.

Efficient product delivery enhancements are also a critical focus. TTI recognizes the importance of not only creating excellent assessment tools but also ensuring they are accessible, user-friendly, and effectively integrated into clients' existing systems and processes. This involves leveraging technology to streamline the delivery and implementation of their assessments, making them more accessible to a wider audience.

Embracing longitudinal continual improvement is a key philosophy for us as well. The original developmental process of our assessments may not completely align with present-day protocols, but it's vital to value our historic journey. This long-term perspective allows us to build on our legacy of innovation, learning from past experiences and adapting our methodologies to meet the demands of the present and future.

> **We recognize that the pursuit of excellence in assessing and understanding human potential is an evolving journey, not a static destination.**

TTI's commitment to revealing human potential is underpinned by a deep investment in research and innovation, continuous scientific validation, the development of new products to meet emerging needs, enhancing the efficiency of product delivery, and a steadfast dedication to continual improvement over time. This multifaceted approach ensures that our tools and methodologies remain at the forefront of the industry, providing invaluable insights into the complexities of human behavior and potential in the workplace.

HISTORY OF TTI SUCCESS INSIGHTS

TTI Success Insights has a fascinating origin story that underscores the power of vision, innovation, and a deep understanding of human potential.

The inception of TTI Success Insights can be traced back to the late 1970s, when Bill, intrigued by what he was observing about people, embarked on a journey to explore the science of human potential and performance. Bill had been a passionate educator and entrepreneur and was intrigued by the idea of using assessments to enhance individual and organizational performance. He believed that a better understanding of individual behaviors, motivators, and skills could transform the way people work and interact.

In the early days, Bill's vision was to create tools that could provide insights into the core behaviors of individuals. He was particularly interested in the DISC theory. Bill saw the potential of applying this theory to the business world, particularly for improving employee selection, development, and retention.

To turn his vision into reality, Bill, his son, Dave, along with other collaborators began developing assessment tools that could accurately measure these behavioral traits. They focused on creating assessments that were not only scientifically valid and reliable but also practical and easy to understand for businesses of all sizes.

One of the early challenges was to create assessments that were applicable to the real-world business environment. The team worked diligently to ensure that their tools were not just theoretical but provided actionable insights that could be used for improving employee engagement, leadership development, team building, and overall organizational effectiveness.

As the company grew, it expanded its portfolio beyond just behavioral assessments. Recognizing that behavior was only one piece of the human potential puzzle, TTI began to develop tools to measure other critical aspects, such as motivators, emotional intelligence, competencies, and acumen. This holistic approach set TTI apart, offering a comprehensive suite of assessments that provided a 360-degree view of an individual's potential.

The 1990s and early 2000s marked a period of significant growth and innovation for the company. TTI Success Insights was among the first in the industry to embrace and integrate technology into their assessment processes. The introduction of online assessments revolutionized how their tools were administered and interpreted, making them more accessible and user-friendly.

Throughout its journey, TTI has remained committed to research and innovation. The company has continuously invested in scientific research to ensure the validity and reliability of its assessments. Collaborations with psychologists, data scientists, and industry experts have been central to their development process.

Today, TTI Success Insights is recognized globally for its expertise in talent management and workforce development. Their tools are used by thousands of organizations worldwide, including Fortune 500 companies, and have been translated into over 40 languages to cater to a global audience.

The legacy of my brother, Bill J. Bonnstetter, lives on through the work of TTI Success Insights. His vision of uncovering human potential and his belief in the transformative power of understanding individual behaviors and motivators continue to be the driving forces behind the company's success. TTI stands as a testament to the impact that a deep understanding of human behavior, combined with innovative technology and a commitment to research, can have on individuals and organizations worldwide.

BACKING UP THE SCIENCES OF SELF WITH SCIENTIFIC PROOF

TTI Success Insights has long been committed to grounding our methodologies in solid scientific research. This commitment is proven through the work we are doing in using evaluation and brain imaging techniques to provide scientific validation for the sciences behind TTI's tools.

The core of TTI's approach lies in understanding and assessing human behaviors, motivators, and skills. This approach is rooted in established psychological theories and models, including assessing behaviors using the DISC theory and the driving forces behind human motivation. However, in the realm of human behavior and psychology, it is not enough to merely base tools on established theories; empirical evidence and ongoing research are crucial for ensuring accuracy, relevance, and effectiveness.

Our work in evaluation and brain imaging has been instrumental in providing this empirical backing. Through sophisticated real-time electroencephalogram (EEG) brain imaging techniques, we have been able to study how the brain responds to different stimuli and trace neurological decision-making pathways. This research has shed light on the brain's response processing that TTI's assessments aim to measure.

The brain imaging process is able to draw from our patented EEG processes to show whether an assessment item is accepted or rejected, as well as the emotional intensity of their reaction. These brain images are then compared to their assessment responses to determine the degree of match. For example, we have discovered and documented that left prefrontal cortex flares of gamma activity are correlated to acceptance and right prefrontal cortex flares are correlated to rejection.

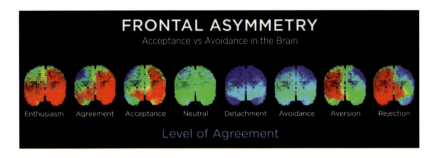

One significant aspect of our research involves understanding how the brain processes information related to behavioral styles and decision-making. This kind of research not only validates the theoretical foundations of the assessments but also provides insights into how these traits manifest in neurological activity.

> **The use of brain imaging in research represents a cutting-edge approach to validating psychological assessments.**

Brain imaging allows for a more nuanced understanding of the complex interplay between brain activity and decisions, going beyond self-reported data and observational studies. This scientific rigor not only enhances the credibility of TTI's tools but also contributes to the broader field of behavioral science.

The scientific proof backing the sciences used by TTI is a testament to the company's commitment to excellence and innovation. By bridging the gap between psychological theories and neurological evidence, we have created a suite of assessment tools that are not only reliable and valid but also continuously evolving with the latest scientific findings. This dedication to scientific validation not only enhances the quality of their assessments but also contributes significantly to the understanding of human behavior in the workplace.

CARISSA'S STORY: HOW BRAIN SCIENCE CAN TRANSFORM

I've always been someone who watches and learns before trying something myself, wanting to get it right the first time. This perfectionism often led to indecision and anxiety about making mistakes or upsetting others. As a child and even into adulthood, I was the one who always followed the rules.

It wasn't until grad school that I took my first personality assessment, which was a real eye-opener. It gave me the language to understand and explain my behavior patterns, and it connected me with others who shared similar traits. It was reassuring to find people like me, but it also helped me to grasp the perspectives of those who were very different. I've never had trouble getting along with others, but I didn't always understand why they acted the way they did. At 23 years old, the assessment taught me a lot about myself, but I didn't fully apply that knowledge in the real world. In my first job, I struggled because I was still approaching work like a school assignment, focusing on perfect execution rather than learning to navigate the complexities of the workplace and office politics.

For three years, I was at that job where, despite working closely with my supervisor, we never connected beyond work tasks. Our office was full of tension, and I was cautious, trying to understand everyone's intentions without overstepping. We even completed a behavioral assessment but never acted on the insights it provided.

Leaving wasn't tough, but it left me questioning my career path. That's when I found a job working for TTI Success Insights. I've always believed in the power of assessments and was thrilled by the prospect of working somewhere that embraced their transformative potential. At TTI, I dove into the science behind the assessments and was captivated by our team's commitment to personal growth and the rigorous research that validated our methods. It's one thing to call these tools behavior tests, but I've learned they're much deeper, grounded in neuroscience, and they reveal the alignment between subconscious reactions and conscious thoughts—a level of insight that's undeniably profound.

Understanding myself better has been a game changer in my interactions with family and colleagues. It's like having insider knowledge that helps me decode our interactions.

My experience in the brain lab last spring was even more eye-opening. I was apprehensive at first, but the brain imaging exercise was a powerful confirmation of the personal healing I'd been working on. It was enlightening to see that words linked to past trauma didn't affect me as strongly as I anticipated, suggesting I had moved past issues more than I had realized.

This realization was liberating, showing me that while I'm still conscious of my past, it no longer has a grip on me. Similarly, positive stimuli that resonated with me on the screen were a joy to acknowledge. It's one thing to feel joy but another to have it confirmed through brain imaging. This level of self-understanding is incredibly validating. And with this knowledge, there's the powerful option to unpack and learn from it.

TTI SUCCESS INSIGHTS' MEASURABLE RESULTS

Beyond the groundbreaking work of brain imaging and evaluation, TTI Success Insights employs a variety of other measurable results and methods to ensure the efficacy and reliability of our assessment tools. These methods are crucial in maintaining the scientific rigor and practical relevance of the products in the dynamic field of human resource management and organizational development.

Statistical Validity and Reliability Testing: TTI rigorously tests our assessments for statistical validity and reliability. This involves ensuring that the assessments consistently measure what they are intended to measure (validity) and produce stable and consistent results over time (reliability). These tests often involve large sample sizes and are repeated periodically to ensure ongoing accuracy.

Behavioral and Psychometric Analysis: TTI uses advanced psychometric techniques to analyze behavioral data. This involves exploring how different personality traits and behaviors correlate with various outcomes in the workplace, such as job performance, team dynamics, and leadership effectiveness.

Feedback from Users and Practitioners: Gathering feedback from those who use our assessments—including HR professionals, coaches, and organizational leaders—is a key part of our approach. This feedback helps in fine-tuning the assessments to better meet the needs of users and to remain relevant to current workplace challenges.

Longitudinal Studies: TTI conducts longitudinal studies to track the long-term effectiveness of our assessments. These studies observe how accurately the assessments predict performance and other outcomes over extended periods.

Benchmarking: TTI often uses benchmarking to compare an individual's assessment results with established norms or standards. This method is particularly useful in organizational settings where specific roles require certain competencies or behavioral traits.

Case Studies and Organizational Outcomes: Real-world case studies are used to demonstrate the impact of our assessments in various organizational contexts. This includes examining how our tools have helped in areas like talent acquisition, employee development, team building, and conflict resolution.

Continuous Improvement Process: TTI implements a continuous improvement process for our assessments, constantly updating them based on new research, technological advancements, and changing workplace trends. This process ensures that our tools remain current and effective.

Cultural and Global Adaptation Studies: Recognizing the importance of cultural context, TTI conducts studies to adapt and validate our assessments for different cultural settings. This ensures that the tools are applicable and reliable across diverse global workforces.

TTI employs a multifaceted approach to validating and enhancing our assessment tools, combining traditional methods of statistical analysis with innovative techniques and real-world feedback. This comprehensive approach ensures that our products not only stand up to scientific scrutiny but also meet the practical needs of modern workplaces around the world.

AMERICAN PSYCHOLOGICAL ASSOCIATION STANDARDS

TTI Success Insights, like many organizations in the field of psychology and behavioral assessment, uses and implements American Psychological Association (APA) standards in our research, reporting, and documentation processes. TTI adheres to APA guidelines in the following ways.

Research publications and white papers: When TTI conducts research studies and publishes findings, we use APA guidelines to format our papers. This includes structuring the paper with a title page, abstract, main body, and references, as well as adhering to the appropriate style for in-text citations and references.

Documentation and reporting: In developing and presenting reports, especially those that involve psychological assessment or data analysis, TTI uses APA format to ensure clarity, professionalism, and standardization.

Ethical guidelines: APA also provides ethical guidelines for psychologists. TTI adheres to these ethical standards in our methodology, particularly regarding participant treatment, consent, and confidentiality.

Academic collaborations: In partnerships with academic institutions or in contexts where our work is subject to academic scrutiny, the use of APA guidelines is essential for maintaining scholarly integrity and ensuring that our work aligns with academic standards.

Response processing: *The APA Handbook of Testing and Assessment in Psychology* states that assessment response processes require the collection of evidence demonstrating that the test taker is cognitively processing and properly interpreting the intended purpose of test items. This form of validation evidence is used to demonstrate that the assessment directs participants to engage in specific behaviors deemed necessary to complete the designed purpose of the assessment items.

The protocol involves collecting electroencephalographic (EEG) data using standardized low-resolution brain electromagnetic tomography (sLORETA) to analyze and view voxel images of real-time brain activity collected while a participant responds to assessment items (voxel is a shortened term for *volume pixel* and is the 3D equivalent of the 2D pixel).

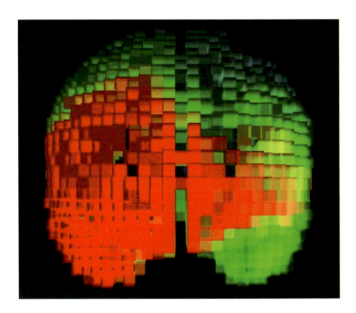

EEG image showing strong rejection of an assessment item.

By collecting images from the moment of stimulus exposure to the moment that the respondent selects a Likert scale answer (a Likert-type scale is a psychometric scale for survey responses that provide multiple levels of agreement to choose from for a specific item or statement), we can gather many insights about the brain's responses to the survey:

- How final answers compare to brain processing data
- Brain decision-making pathways when exposed to reverse or double negative assessment items
- Exposure of brain processing when faced with socially loaded statements
- Resulting brain processing of neutrally scored stimulus

The collected data must be correlated against quantitative item analysis of population data, such as inter-item correlations and item factor loading based on exploratory factor analysis, to reveal how the brain responds to these stimuli.

In general, adherence to APA guidelines in such contexts not only ensures consistency and professionalism but also enhances the credibility and acceptance of our work within the academic and professional communities.

TTI SUCCESS INSIGHTS INTO THE FUTURE

It's clear that Bill's vision has grown into a formidable enterprise that not only cherishes its roots but also eagerly embraces the future. The company's steadfast dedication to unlocking human potential through the Science of Self™ has set a new standard in the realm of assessments. This journey, marked by a commitment to research, innovation, and the relentless pursuit of excellence, reflects a deep understanding that the quest to comprehend and enhance human potential is never-ending.

Looking ahead, TTI Success Insights is poised to navigate the complexities of the future with the same fervor and dedication that have characterized its past. As the company continues to refine its existing tools and develop new ones in response to the dynamic demands of the global workforce, it remains committed to making these assessments more accessible and integrated into the fabric of organizational and individual development. This forward-thinking approach, coupled with respect for the journey thus far, ensures that TTI will continue to offer invaluable insights and tools for understanding human behavior and potential. We are left with a sense of anticipation for what the future holds, not just for the company but for the broader field of human potential and workplace dynamics.

THE SCIENCE OF DISC

Understanding human behavior, especially in the context of diverse behavioral styles and attitudes, is a fundamental pursuit in both psychology and business. Within this realm, the DISC assessment tool emerges as a critical bridge linking personal characteristics with professional behavior. Based on the psychological theories of William Moulton Marston and Prescott Lecky, DISC categorizes behavior into four primary types or dimensions:

- Dominance—how you respond to problems and challenges
- Influence—how you respond to people and contacts
- Steadiness—how you respond to pace and consistency in your environment
- Compliance—how you respond to procedures and constraints

The core concept of DISC involves understanding how the four behavioral factors (dimensions) work together to create an individual's unique behavioral style profile. While a typical person may have one or two primary behavioral characteristics, the combination of tendencies for all four dimensions defines a person's behavioral style more accurately than simply identifying a single highest score.

Within each dimension, a person's behavioral style will fall somewhere on the spectrum of possibilities, and when a person's tendencies fall at one extreme, those tendencies are identified as a primary behavioral style. Each dimension will reveal two possible primary behavioral styles for a total of eight styles.

For many years, these eight styles were referred to as "high" or "low" behavioral styles based on DISC assessment scores from 0-100 in each dimension. In 2020, TTI introduced the Behavioral Continuum concept, which reconfigures each dimension to a horizontal continuum graph that displayed the two extreme styles at the right and left. Scores were converted to show results from 50-100 at one end or the other of each dimension, eliminating the "high" and "low" terms and any assumption of a style that was lacking in some feature or importance. In 2024, TTI more formally introduced the Behavioral Continuum. They began training TTI partners on how to exchange the traditional vertical graphs used to display assessment results with the horizontal continuums graphs in their book *Introducing the DISC Continuum.*

The eight behavioral styles are described below:

- Dominance dimension – **direct**: Addresses problems & challenges in an aggressive, straightforward manner without changing direction or stopping until they are solved (formerly "high D," the right side of the Continuum)

- Dominance dimension – **reflective**: Addresses problems & challenges purposefully with a contemplative, deliberate, and thoughtful style (formerly "low D," the left side of the Continuum)

- Influence dimension – **outgoing**: Addresses people & contacts with an open, lively, optimistic, and approachable communication style (formerly "high I," the right side of the Continuum)

- Influence dimension – **reserved**: Addresses people & contacts with a quiet, realistic, and pragmatic style (formerly "low I," the left side of the Continuum)

- Steadiness dimension – **steady**: Addresses pace & consistency in a predictable, consistent, and patient way (formerly "high S," the right side of the Continuum)

- Steadiness dimension – **dynamic**: Addresses pace & consistency with a more variable, versatile, quick, and excited approach (formerly "low S," the left side of the Continuum)

- Compliance dimension – **rigorous**: Works with procedures & constraints by first finding the established rules and procedures and then applying them (formerly "high C," the right side of the Continuum)

- Compliance dimension – **experiential**: Approaches procedures & constraints with a more spontaneous, experimental, trial-and-error style (formerly "low C," the left side of the Continuum)

The closer a person's DISC score is to one extreme is expressed as intensity—that is, the farther their score is from the midline, a score of 50, the stronger their tendency to display that behavior will be. The most extreme tendencies, the scores farthest from the midline in one or sometimes two dimensions, are the primary behavioral styles they will display.

These traits go beyond mere behaviors; they shape complex emotional and interpersonal dynamics. For example, people with a direct primary style often display self-confidence and a competitive streak. Those with an outgoing primary style value social interactions and collaboration. People with steady primary style prefer stability and show patience, whereas rigorous individuals are detail-oriented and rule-abiding. Understanding these traits allows for better predictions of responses in various situations, communication preferences, and motivational triggers. It also allows a person to know where their natural tendencies will be an advantage and where they may need to adapt their behavior or where they may be uncomfortable or at a disadvantage.

> **Behavioral research suggests that the most effective people are those who understand both their strengths and weaknesses.**

These people can best develop strategies to meet the demands of their environment. In essence, they are more self-aware. Self-awareness can be broadly defined as the extent to which people are consciously aware of their internal states and interactions or relationships with others.[1]

It is also important to recognize that most successful people can identify their strengths but may be oblivious to their weaknesses,[2] thus another reason to employ assessments.

Behavior is an integral aspect of our identity, representing the observable aspects of human actions. The four dimensions of DISC provide a comprehensive view of how an individual operates within different contexts.

---

1. Trudeau K.J., and R. Reich. (1995). Correlates of psychological mindedness. *Personality and Individual Differences*, 19(5), 699–704: https://www.sciencedirect.com/science/article/abs/pii/019188699500110R; Brown, K.W., and R.M. Ryan. (2003). The benefits of being present: mindfulness and its role in psychological well-being. *Journal of Personality and Social Psychology*, 84(4), 822-48: https://pubmed.ncbi.nlm.nih.gov/12703651/

2. Zenger, J., and J. Folkman. Why the Most Productive People Don't Always Make the Best Managers. Harvard Business Review, April 17, 2018: https://karokasb.org/wp-content/uploads/2018/08/Why-the-Most-Productive-People-Don%E2%80%99t-Always-Make-the-Best-Managers.pdf

THE POWER OF DISC

The power of understanding and utilizing DISC can be found in numerous settings. For example, a college basketball coach successfully employed TTI behavioral styles with his team members to increase the odds of winning. As a team-building activity, the coach had all his players and coaches take the DISC assessment. He then asked them to share their DISC profiles. The coach used this information to create his starting teams. This became even more important as the games progressed and required different team dynamics.

Using DISC profiles, the coach had very specific plays: "One of my strategies is that if we are ahead by six or more points and with less than two minutes to play, I pull all of my players with a direct style off the court and replace them with players with a more steady style. I can't afford to have risk-taking screw up our lead."

Understanding the characteristics of different styles allows businesses to put the right people in a job and allows for teams to be able to maximize collaboration.

THE HISTORY OF DISC

An in-depth history of the development and application of the DISC model is part of TTI's DISC technical manual, *Style Insights® Technical Manual Version 1.0*.[3] Highlights from the history of DISC provide a sense of important contributions that have been made in the field.

---

3. Gehrig, E., Ph.D., and R. Bonnstetter, Ph.D. *TTI Success Insights Style Insights® Technical Manual Version 1.0* (TTI Success Insights, 2021): https://images.ttisi.com/wp-content/uploads/research/2022/05/03132738/R4techman_2021_v01.pdf

William Marston's Work in the 1920s and DISC Theory

William Marston was a man of diverse interests and talents. He was a well-known psychologist, as well as the creator of *Wonder Woman*, a film writer, and the inventor of the systolic blood pressure test, which was an early component of the modern polygraph test. His work in the early 20th century significantly impacted both psychological theory and practical applications in the field. However, his most enduring contribution to psychology was the DISC theory.

Marston's DISC model was groundbreaking in providing a framework for understanding human behavior with greater detail and understanding. He believed that individuals exhibit one of the DISC traits more prominently than others and that this shapes their interactions with their environment and the people around them.

Marston believed that these behavioral traits could be known and understood to improve relationships and workplace productivity. He suggested that understanding a person's DISC profile could lead to better job placement, improved workplace communication, and more effective management strategies.

While Marston is widely recognized for developing the DISC theory, his influence extends beyond this. He also developed an early version of the lie detector based on his theory that blood pressure changes are linked to emotional states, such as lying. This invention showcased his belief that the psyche could influence the physical body.

Marston's theories on emotions and behavior also had implications outside of the psychological community. His ideas influenced his creation of the *Wonder Woman* comic book character in the 1940s. He created her with the four DISC traits: dominance, influence, steadfastness, and a compliant adherence to a moral code. *Wonder*

Woman was also a reflection of Marston's progressive attitudes toward women during that era.

Despite the initial skepticism, Marston's DISC theory endured. It was soon adopted and adapted for practical use by students and colleagues of Marston.

Prescott Lecky

Prescott Lecky was a colleague of William Moulton Marston. While Marston is credited with formulating the DISC theory, Lecky's contributions were almost more significant in the early development and application of the concepts underlying the model. Lecky worked with Marston at Columbia University and was instrumental in furthering the practical applications of Marston's theoretical framework, particularly in educational and counseling settings.

Lecky's work with Marston during the 1920s and 1930s focused on understanding the psychological phenomena of self-help, self-regulation, and self-concept. This new theory was built on the belief that the most important motivator was the preservation of the self-image. He understood that what one believes about oneself dictates their behavior. These concepts are critical in the DISC model, which assesses how individuals regulate their behavior in response to the environment and their self-perception. Lecky's insights helped to expand the DISC theory beyond a simple categorization of personal traits, suggesting that a person's self-concept can greatly influence how they exhibit dominance, influence, steadiness, and compliance.

In educational psychology, Lecky's emphasis on self-concept aligned with the DISC principles to suggest that students have unique emotional and behavioral profiles that can impact their learning and social interactions. His ideas contributed to shaping personalized teaching approaches and understanding behavior. This was a precursor to recognizing the importance of catering to individual student needs, a fundamental aspect of modern educational practices.

Although Lecky may not be as widely recognized as Marston, his role in refining and applying the DISC model was a cornerstone in its historical development. The collaboration between Marston and Lecky exemplifies the early interdisciplinary work in psychology that combined research with practical application. This trend has continued to shape the field to this day.

Walter Clarke

Walter Clarke emerged as a key figure in advancing DISC theory by connecting it with real-world uses. Clarke studied under both Marston and Lecky and though he chose different wording to pinpoint the meaning of the four vectors, he combined their pioneering psychological understandings into an actionable and measurable assessment tool known as the Activity Vector Analysis (AVA). The AVA became fundamental in personal attributes evaluations within businesses and organizations, leading to new insights into workforce behavior and management tactics.

While Marston's and Lecky's work was insightful, Walter Clarke recognized that it lacked a solid way to measure the DISC traits within individuals. He saw the potential for practical application in the workplace, where understanding an individual's behavioral tendencies could significantly affect their role and performance within a team or organization.

Walter Clarke was able to significantly advance the practical application of Marston's DISC theory through his work with the

United States Air Force. As a psychologist in a military setting, Clarke was presented with a unique and structured environment to observe a wide array of behaviors and personal attribute types. This exposure was instrumental in shaping his understanding and application of DISC theory, particularly in personnel assessment and team dynamics.

> **In the Air Force, where team cohesion and effective leadership are crucial, Clarke's use of DISC theory helped categorize and understand the behavioral styles of personnel, thereby enhancing team efficiency and communication.**

Clarke's role allowed him to develop practical tools and methodologies based on the DISC model. He created assessment tools that were straightforward to administer and interpret, and tailored for the hierarchical and systematic nature of the military. These tools were integrated into training and development programs, educating leaders and team members about different personal attribute styles and improving interactions within diverse teams. His work also involved extensive data collection and analysis, providing a rich source of information to refine and validate the DISC theory. This research was key in adapting the theory to be more relevant and applicable in predicting behaviors and improving team functionality.

His successful application and adaptation of DISC theory in the challenging environment of the Air Force not only validated its utility but also paved the way for its broader application in various sectors.

Clarke meticulously fashioned the AVA, a questionnaire that translated the DISC theory into specific behaviors that people could identify with or not, giving a numeric value to the DISC traits. He employed rigor when developing the assessments to ensure credibility and establish transparency.

The AVA gave a way to objectively look at someone's primary characteristics, offering a predictive glimpse of their reactions in various scenarios. This approach changed the corporate sector, which typically relied on gut feelings when making staffing decisions.

> **The AVA questionnaire was among the first methods using self-evaluation to measure personal traits, pioneering the practical application of psychology in a measurable form.**

Companies started to apply the AVA for many purposes, like improving hiring by finding applicants whose behavior matched the job, promoting the right people into leadership, and fine-tuning team dynamics for better overall performance.

The debut of the AVA signified a turn in human resources (HR) methods, promoting decisions based on solid psychological data instead of just instinct. Clarke's AVA highlighted the relevance of personal attributes in the workplace, showing that job success and satisfaction often depend on how closely a person's behavior aligns with the demands of their job and with the company's culture.

Clarke also helped normalize the use of psychological evaluations at work, advancing the notion that these tools were useful not just for hiring but for employee growth. Managers and leaders started to adjust their approaches based on AVA results to meet their teams' needs better, leading to more supportive and efficient workplaces.

Clarke's influence remains significant, with the AVA setting the stage for the many personal attribute tests now integral on a global scale to staff development, team building, and leadership training.

Beyond his contribution to advancing personal attribute tests, Clarke desired to use his company to change the world for the better. He chose not to patent any of his work and had no objections to other people using his ideas because he wanted to create the most good he could in the world.

Clarke's contributions have had a lasting impact on organizational psychology and leadership development, demonstrating the practical utility of DISC theory in diverse and dynamic settings. His work set a precedent for the use of psychological theories in real-world environments, underscoring the importance of adaptable and practical approaches in the field of industrial psychology.

John P. Cleaver

John "Clipper" Cleaver was another pivotal figure in the evolution of the DISC personal attributes assessment model. His work in the latter half of the 20th century expanded on the theoretical foundations laid by Marston and Lecky. Cleaver's influence, like Clarke's, was transformative, bridging the gap between academic theory and practical application in the corporate world.

Cleaver's interest in DISC began with his exposure to Clarke's Activity Vector Analysis. While Clarke's tool had made significant strides in making the DISC theory operational within a professional setting, Cleaver foresaw the model's broader potential. In the 1970s, he started his own company with the specific goal of developing a DISC-based profile assessment that was more accessible and actionable for the average person, not just psychologists.

Cleaver's innovation was the creation of a self-interpretable DISC assessment. This meant that individuals could take the assessment and immediately understand the results without the need for intermediaries. His approach allowed individuals and managers to directly engage with the material and apply it to their personal and professional development.

The Cleaver version of the DISC test was revolutionary, offering straightforward, immediate insights into a person's primary and secondary personality aspects within the DISC categories. It didn't just categorize personality traits; it provided practical tips on how to utilize one's strengths and adapt to compensate for weaker areas.

Cleaver didn't limit the use of DISC to employee selection and development; he expanded it to team building, conflict management, and enhancing communication at work. With his guidance, DISC became a key resource for understanding team dynamics, preventing and addressing conflicts, and strengthening group efficiency.

> **Cleaver believed that grasping different personality types was essential for better teamwork and leadership within any organization.**

Cleaver's model also greatly impacted sales training. Sales professionals could use their DISC insights to identify clients' personalities and tailor their approach, leading to better communication, stronger customer relationships, and more effective sales methods.

Cleaver's imprint on the DISC framework had widespread effects, integrating the tool into global corporate training programs. The widespread use of DISC, with millions of assessments conducted each year, owes a lot to Cleaver's efforts. His work didn't just make DISC broadly accessible; it became an essential tool for personal and organizational progress.

John G. Geier, Ph.D.

John G. Geier, Ph.D., stands as the next force in the advancement and spread of the DISC personality assessment. In the early 1970s, he, along with a group of innovators, helped develop Performax Systems International, Inc., a frontrunner in marketing and HR that helped to refine and distribute the DISC tool more widely.

Geier leveraged his scholarly expertise and research acumen to scientifically shore up the DISC assessment, bolstering its reliability and precision. His rendition of the DISC tool was crafted for user-friendliness with a clear emphasis on practicality within the professional realm. Geier and Performax Systems International implemented a multilevel marketing approach in the late 1970s and was sold to Carlson Marketing Group soon after.

Guided by Geier, the DISC assessment transcended its original form as a mere behavioral style quiz. It became an extensive framework aimed at boosting workplace efficiency, advancing communication, and aiding in team cohesion. The tool offered insights into the varied behavioral styles of individuals, providing a blueprint for leveraging these differences to enhance teamwork and leadership in companies.

The collective endeavor of Geier and Carlson Marketing Group led to the DISC model's broad implementation across different sectors in the form of a very practical DISC product called the Personal Profile System™. It became instrumental not only in personal growth but also in corporate strategies for leadership training, sales enhancement, and customer service. The DISC model was integrated into numerous corporate training initiatives, cultivating a deeper mutual understanding among staff and executives, which contributed to more productive and agreeable work settings.

Bill J. Bonnstetter and TTI Success Insights

Bill embarked on his academic journey at Iowa State Teachers College. There, he earned a bachelor's degree in business, focusing on marketing in 1964. His thirst for knowledge led him to attain a master's degree in business education in 1969 from the University of Northern Iowa. Fueled by a deep-seated desire to help people understand themselves better, Bill joined forces with Carlson Marketing Group in the late 1970s.

As mentioned earlier, Bill was driven to conduct his own research for deeper insights, and he initiated a unique study involving Midwestern farmers. He utilized the DISC assessment to analyze their buying styles and meticulously documented each farmstead through photographs. This documentation included images of their farm buildings, equipment choices and conditions, access lanes, and other observable elements linked to the farmers' behavioral styles. Bill's innovative approach successfully correlated visual cues of the farmsteads with primary DISC behavioral styles, providing groundbreaking insights.

In 1984, a significant advancement came when Bill's son, David Bonnstetter, brought his computer programming expertise to the table. Their collaboration led to the development of the first computerized DISC behavioral assessment and personalized report. That year marked another milestone when Bill and David co-founded Target Training International, Ltd., which later became TTI Success Insights, further cementing their legacy in the field of behavioral assessments.

Bill and Dave significantly advanced the application of DISC assessments in the professional world through TTI, which focused on enhancing talent management and personal assessment methodologies. Bill's introduction to DISC in the 1980s marked the beginning of a transformative journey in human resource development, where he envisioned the DISC model as a critical tool for delving into the intricacies of human behavior and bolstering workplace efficacy.

TTI became renowned for crafting a series of multifaceted assessment tools that synergized DISC with other behavioral and motivational models. This strategic integration resulted in a robust analytical framework that allowed for an in-depth exploration of an individual's behavior (through DISC), intrinsic motivators (driving forces), and skill set (competencies). By implementing such a comprehensive approach, the powerful combination of assessments evolved into a nuanced instrument that elucidated the how, why, and what of individual actions and potential.

Bill's pioneering strategy of merging the DISC framework with additional evaluative components distinguished TTI's assessments for their complexity and actionable insights. His innovative method facilitated a multilayered understanding of personal and professional traits, which proved invaluable in a variety of applications such as leadership development, team building, and talent acquisition. TTI, under his guidance, did not merely aim to chart behavioral types but sought to leverage that understanding to forge substantial advancements in communication, teamwork, and job satisfaction.

The reach of Bill and Dave's work was vast, with TTI's DISC assessments gaining traction across the globe as a pivotal resource for personal growth and organizational enhancement. The assessments were not static; they were dynamically crafted to cater to the unique needs of diverse sectors, including corporate enterprises, educational institutions, and individual consultancies. TTI's commitment to ongoing research and innovation meant that DISC assessments under his banner were continuously refined, ensuring their relevance and efficacy in an ever-evolving professional landscape.

Furthermore, Bill's legacy is deeply ingrained in the educational content and certification courses offered by TTI Success Insights. He championed disseminating knowledge and expertise concerning DISC assessments through comprehensive training programs. These initiatives were designed to empower coaches, trainers, and consultants with the proficiency required to deploy DISC assessments effectively. Bill's foresight in creating these educational pathways ensured that the benefits of DISC assessments were maximized, fostering a widespread understanding of their practical utility.

Bill J. Bonnstetter's contributions have made a lasting impact on the field of DISC assessment and its application in the real world. Through TTI, he provided tools that were not only rooted in rigorous scientific principles but were also attuned to the practical demands of the modern workplace. His holistic view of personal assessment has enriched the professional journeys of countless individuals and has significantly shaped the discourse on talent management and organizational success.

THE FUTURE OF DISC

In my time with TTI Success Insights, I've had the humbling opportunity to contribute to a fascinating intersection of disciplines, marrying the nuanced world of DISC behavioral assessments with the empirical rigor of brain imaging. This journey has been less about pioneering work and more about listening closely to what the data—both psychological and neurological—tell us about human behavior.

My role primarily involved leveraging technologies like electroencephalography (EEG) to peek into the brain's workings, with the hope of understanding how various DISC personality types manifest at a neurological level. It's been a learning process, one where every pattern or anomaly revealed by the EEG readings brought us a step closer to appreciating the complexity of human nature.

The findings from this research suggested that different DISC profiles might indeed have distinct brain wave patterns. For instance, someone with a strong primary direct style (formerly "high D") might exhibit a particular neural pattern when making decisions. In contrast, a person with a strong primary steady style (formerly "high S") might show different activity under the same conditions. This wasn't about proving a theory but about seeing confirmation in the rich tapestry of brain activity.

While correlating unique brain activity to each DISC style has not been established, response processing using brain activity has shown that each style responds differently to assessment descriptive words.

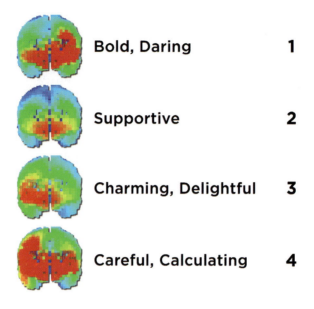

This figure compares an assessment taker's rank ordering of the listed four choices, with 1 being the "most like me" and 4 being the "least." On the left are the brain images captured at the moment of decision-making. While this is only one cell from the behavioral assessment, the completed assessment report identified this person as a primary direct style ("high D") with their next strongest intensity as experiential ("low C"). Note how the brain image regarding acceptance and rejection align with their D and C dimension word choices.

At TTI Success Insights, our goal has always been to refine and improve our tools for the betterment of workplace dynamics and personal growth. By understanding the brain's role in these behavioral traits, we aimed to create more precise assessments. It's been a collective effort, one that involved many talented individuals whose insights and hard work were the true drivers of progress.

The practical applications of this research have been particularly rewarding. Recognizing that tailored training programs could be developed from these insights has been a gratifying realization.

THE SCIENCE OF DISC

> **It's one thing to develop theories; it's another thing entirely to see them enhance someone's personal or professional life.**

I've also found great value in sharing our research with the wider academic community. It's never been just about what these findings mean for TTI Success Insights but also about their potential to contribute to the broader understanding of how we, as individuals, function and interact.

Looking back, it's clear that any advancements made were the result of standing on the shoulders of giants—those who built the theoretical foundations of the DISC assessments and those who pioneered the use of EEG in scientific inquiry. I've simply had the privilege of being part of the conversation, one that explores how personality traits might be reflected in the very fibers of our being.

In reflecting on this work, I'm reminded that the science itself, not the scientist, should be at the forefront. It's about what we can learn and how we can apply that knowledge compassionately and thoughtfully. The integration of brain imaging with DISC assessments is just one small chapter in the vast narrative of understanding the human condition. This narrative continues to inspire and challenge us all.

WHAT YOU SHOULD KNOW ABOUT DISC
by Carissa

DISC is the foundational model for many behavioral theories and is a great starting point for anyone new to self-assessment. It simplifies the complex world of behaviors, making it easier to recognize and understand them. For those unaccustomed to introspection, DISC provides a basic structure for understanding both your own actions and those of others, which is crucial for adapting effectively in a professional environment. It offers a way to categorize and comprehend behaviors in a clear, relatable manner. By grasping the behavioral dynamics that each person contributes, you can better navigate team interactions and collaborations.

THE SCIENCE OF MOTIVATION

The science of motivation is an intriguing field that bridges psychology, neurology, and sociology to comprehend what propels individuals to take action. While DISC offers insights into *how* someone will behave, motivators and driving forces explain the *why*.

At its core, motivation refers to the processes that guide, energize, and sustain behaviors aimed at achieving goals. This multifaceted discipline seeks to decode the intricacies of human desire and drive, examining both the internal and external factors that prompt individuals to move toward specific objectives.

Understanding motivation is instrumental in deciphering personality and predicting behavior. Personalities are largely shaped by the kinds of motives that individuals prioritize, whether they seek achievement, power, affiliation, or other incentives. The force of motivation influences not only what people do but how they think and feel about their actions, thus offering a comprehensive understanding of their behavioral patterns. For instance, an individual driven by achievement may consistently seek out challenges and opportunities for success, while someone motivated by affiliation might prioritize social relationships and community involvement.

> **We can begin to unlock the secrets behind human action and inaction by delving into the science of motivation.**

This knowledge empowers psychologists, educators, employers, and even individuals to foster environments that enhance motivation. In educational settings, understanding students' motivational drivers can lead to tailored teaching methods that boost engagement and learning. In the workplace, leaders can use motivational science to design incentive systems that align with employees' intrinsic and extrinsic motivators, thereby enhancing productivity and satisfaction.

Because the study of motivation has fascinated humans for centuries, many attempts have been made by philosophers, scholars, and scientists to understand fundamental theories that expose why people respond so differently when confronted with similar situations and stimuli.

Eduard Spranger first defined six primary types or categories to define human motivation and drive:

- Theoretical
- Utilitarian
- Aesthetic
- Social
- Individualistic
- Traditional

With TTI Success Insights' additional understanding of Spranger's original work, the 12 Driving Forces® assessment came to life.

The 12 Driving Forces™ are established by looking at each motivator on a continuum and describing both ends. The twelve forces, or descriptors, are based on six keywords, one for each continuum. The six keywords are knowledge, utility, surroundings, others, power, and methodologies.

The goal of this assessment tool is to explain, clarify, and amplify some of the driving forces in your life. The resulting report will empower you to build on the unique strengths that you bring to both work and life. You will learn how your passions from the 12 Driving Forces™ frame your perspectives, providing the most accurate understanding of you as a unique person.

UNDERSTANDING MOTIVATION TO PREDICT ACADEMIC PERFORMANCE IN SURGICAL TRAINING

There are some fascinating applications to understanding what motivates people. A surprising one came about in the medical industry.

The National Science Foundation funded a five-year project to understand and reduce the dropout rate of surgical residents who had made it through the first two to three years of residency but then dropped out in one of the last two years.

The question they pursued was this: *Why* did these residents decide to drop out? The study hypothesis can be found in their initial project publication, quoted here:[4]

---

4. Bell, R.M., S.A. Fann, J.E. Morrison, and J.R. Lisk. (2011). Determining personal talents and behavioral styles of applicants to surgical training: a new look at an old problem, part I. *Journal of Surgical Education*, 68(6), 534-541: https://www.sciencedirect.com/science/article/abs/pii/S193172041100167X; also see Bell, R.M., S.A. Fann, J.E. Morrison, and J.R. Lisk. (2012). Determining personal talents and behavioral styles of applicants to surgical training: a new look at an old problem, part II. *Journal of Surgical Education*, 69(1), 23-29: https://www.sciencedirect.com/science/article/abs/pii/S1931720411001681

> "Resident selection is a difficult process. Traditional methodologies for identifying compatibility between residents and programs are fraught with errors that can prove to be disruptive, costly, and can result in personal and professional setbacks for applicant residents. Our hypothesis was that the TriMetrix (TTI) System in conjunction with other criteria would be helpful in selecting residents who could be easily integrated into our program and its culture."

Three extensive publications were written related to the project and one of the major findings was tied directly to the role of motivation in program completion. Those who were identified as having a theoretical motivation were more likely *not* to complete their residency.

The final paper documenting the study stated this conclusion:[5]

> "For the senior data group, it was found that . . . increasing Theoretical scores yields a decreasing likelihood of a passing in the examination."

A person with a strong **theoretical** motivation is described in the 12 Driving Forces™ assessment as someone who values knowledge and views its pursuit as a purpose in itself: The world is observed objectively by this person in an attempt to find order in it and identify the systems under which it operates. Knowledge is sought for its own sake, not for any economic benefit or application. The theoretical individual is often considered an intellectual and values knowledge.

---

5. Yost, M.J., Ph.D., J. Gardner, M.S., R. McMurtry Bell, M.D., S.A. Fann, M.D., J.R. Lisk, B.A.; for the TriMetrix and Success Research Group: W.G. Cheadle, M.D., M.H. Goldman, M.D., S. Rawn, R.N., J.A. Weigelt, M.D., P.M. Termuhlen, M.D., R.J. Woods, M.D., E.D. Endean, M.D., J. Kimbrough, R.N., and M. Hulme, M.D. (2015). Predicting Academic Performance in Surgical Training. *Journal of Surgical Education*, 72 (3), 491-499: https://www.sciencedirect.com/science/article/abs/pii/S1931720414003158

THE SCIENCE OF MOTIVATION

In other words, as training progressed into the third and fourth years, highly theoretical residents were faced with a career that required precise replication of techniques, not the pursuit of new knowledge. The first couple of years met their need for learning, but they were not excited about doing this task repeatedly, day after day, for the rest of their professional lives.

Current research is crystal clear regarding the role of purpose in our lives, and identifying what motivates an individual is key to finding purpose.

While not discussed in any of the project's three publications, as an educator of over 40 years, I see another takeaway that is not mentioned. If we look at the characteristics of those residents who left surgery in years three and four, one might conclude that these seven preparation programs were not accommodating to the needs of the dropout audience.

What if a portion of the residency curriculum was designed to offer insights into innovation, curiosity, questioning, and procedural exploration? Do we need some surgeons who push the envelope? Do we need programs that go beyond the traditional procedures and explore new futures? Where do these individuals get that kind of support and training?

Understanding the science of motivation can help us answer these questions and lead to a future full of possibilities.

THE HISTORY OF THE SCIENCE OF MOTIVATION

The science of motivation has a long and involved history. The earliest known writings that could imply aspects of motivation are found in cuneiform, which is one of the oldest writing systems in the world, dating back to before 3000 B.C. The cuneiform script contains over

800 signs, each with multiple meanings. Through these signs, we can discern primitive associations and thought processes that reflect motivational factors, such as the need for food or social connection. However, it wasn't until more modern writings that motivation was directly discussed.

The Ancients: Socrates, Plato, and Aristotle

The ancient philosophers Socrates, Plato, and Aristotle each had profound insights into human nature and motivation, asking, "Why do we do what we do?" These men offered perspectives that continue to influence modern thought. Their exploration of motivation delved into understanding the driving forces behind human actions, desires, and ethical conduct.

Socrates (470–399 B.C.): A major figure in Western philosophy, Socrates believed that knowing yourself is crucial to understanding your desires and motivations. His famous saying, "Know thyself," implies that self-awareness leads to understanding our actions. Socrates thought knowledge and virtue were key motivators for people. He argued that if people understood what was good, they would naturally do good things. So, in his view, doing something wrong results from not understanding what is right. This judgment about what is good compels an intellectual view of motivation and contains reasoning, choosing, and decision-making.

Plato (427–347 B.C.): Socrates' student, Plato built on these ideas. In *The Republic*, he talked about the soul having three parts: the rational, the spirited, and the appetitive. The rational part seeks knowledge and wisdom, the spirited part deals with emotions and honor, and the appetitive part concerns desires and basic needs. Plato said that to live a good and just life, these parts of the soul need to be in balance, with the rational part in charge. When these parts are not balanced, it creates internal conflict, affecting our decisions and actions. For Plato, the highest goal is to seek the form of the *good*, a perfect idea of goodness that goes beyond everyday experiences.

Aristotle (384–322 B.C.): A student of Plato, Aristotle had a more practical approach to motivation. In his *Nicomachean Ethics*, he introduced the idea of "telos," or purpose. Aristotle believed everything has a purpose, and for humans, the ultimate goal is to achieve eudaimonia, which means flourishing or well-being. This is done by practicing virtues, which are habits that help us reach our potential. Aristotle saw motivation as the desire to reach this state of eudaimonia. He believed that people want to do what they think is good, but they need the right moral education and habits to truly understand and achieve this.

These ancient philosophers' ideas form an important base for our understanding of why people act the way they do, and these ideas are still relevant in modern discussions about psychology and philosophy.

The Grand Theories of Motivation

Drawing on the ideas of the ancient philosophers, more modern philosophers sought to discover a **grand theory of motivation** that would provide an overarching theoretical framework to understand human motivation completely. They hoped that this grand theory would unite all the teachings and understanding for all people and situations. Many fundamental truths came out of this search, but none were able to solve the motivational puzzle completely.

These theories, developed by some of the most influential thinkers in psychology and philosophy, offer diverse and profound insights into what drives human actions. The four grand theories of motivation that follow encompass a range of perspectives that have significantly influenced our understanding of human behavior and motivation.

Theory of will: Before he died in 1650 at age 54, René Descartes built on Aristotle's theories, suggesting that while our bodies are simply motivated, our will steers our motivation. Known for his math and philosophy work, Descartes also explored the origins of thought. In the posthumously published *Treatise of Man*, Descartes pinpointed the pineal gland as the soul's home and the birthplace of thoughts—central to our will.

Descartes saw the will as the master of the body's instincts, capable of opposing our natural tendencies. He proposed that understanding motivation was really about understanding the will, a concept that led to two centuries of scholarly work. The notion of *will* as a choice-making force involving effort and resistance was explored by thinkers like Ruckmick and Rand but remained enigmatic. As TTI Success Insights delves into how our brains make decisions, these early explorations into the brain's role in motivation are particularly relevant. This theme of will persists in today's motivation theories, recognizing that will might be revealed through actions that follow thought and planning.

Instinct theory: Descartes believed our will influences our motivation on a purely thought-based level. On the other hand, Darwin, through his observations of ants and other insects, proposed that our actions are influenced by natural instincts. This idea transformed motivation studies from abstract philosophy into a field that's more about biology and science.

William James, an influential American psychologist and philosopher, was one of the leading thinkers of the late 19th century and is often referred to as the "father of American psychology." James contributed significantly to developing psychological and philosophical thought, including the theory of pragmatism and functionalism in psychology. His work on instinct theory included the idea that human behavior is often the result of instincts triggered by specific external stimuli. For example, cats are observed to chase mice; therefore, when a mouse (stimulus) is presented to a cat, the cat will chase it (response).

William McDougall expanded on instinct theory by suggesting that instincts are the driving forces that push people toward specific goals, shedding light on the purposeful nature of human actions. He started to catalog basic human instincts such as exploration, combat, and parenting. However, over time, as the list of these instincts swelled to thousands, it became apparent that they were describing behaviors rather than explaining them. The theoretical foundation was called into question due to its circular reasoning. It was eventually discarded, although the field of evolutionary psychology continues to explore how genetics might influence human behavior.

Staying close to the main topic, it's pertinent to delve a bit into genetics. Establishing a foundational understanding of recent genetic discoveries is crucial for the evolution of self-reporting assessment tools. This includes recognizing how these genetic insights shape human behavior. Kathryn Hall, from Harvard University's Department of Medicine, has made significant contributions through her research on the catechol-O-methyltransferase (COMT) gene and its effect on the placebo response.[6] COMT plays a key role in dopamine regulation, leading to genetically influenced variations in mood, stress

---

6. Hall, K.T., A.J. Lembo, I. Kirsch, D.C. Ziogas, J. Douaiher, K.B. Jensen, L.A. Conboy, J.M. Kelley, E. Kokkotou, and T.J. Kaptchuk. (2012). Catechol-O-Methyltransferase val-158met Polymorphism Predicts Placebo Effect in Irritable Bowel Syndrome. *PLoS One* 7(10), e48135: https://www.ncbi.nlm.nih.gov/pmc/articles/PMC3479140/

response, and openness to suggestions. As such research progresses, it becomes increasingly important to develop personal assessment tools to integrate knowledge from these related areas of study.

Drive theory: In 1918, Robert S. Woodworth introduced the term *drive* to explain instinct theory, somewhat revisiting Aristotle's idea of a three-tiered hierarchy of needs: nutritive, sensitive, and rational. Drive theory is rooted in the biological functions that behaviors serve—essentially, behaviors arise from the body's needs. When there's a disruption in the body's stable state, actions are taken to correct this and return to equilibrium. This physical imbalance is experienced mentally as a "drive."

Sigmund Freud adopted the drive theory, offering a four-part mechanism consisting of source, impetus, object, and aim. He posited that a physical lack, such as thirst, triggers psychological discomfort, leading to anxiety. To alleviate this, one would seek something in the environment, like water, to satisfy the need and calm the anxiety. However, Freud's theory didn't fully account for how learning and experience shape motivation and was based mainly on observations of mentally disturbed patients. Due to these limitations, the theory was eventually replaced by more comprehensive drive theories.

In 1943, Clark Hull proposed a drive reduction theory suggesting that the sum of bodily deficits creates a total need, serving as the primary motivation source. Hull's approach, innovative for its time, aimed to predict motivation and influenced the creation of motivational assessments. He suggested that actions reducing bodily needs lead to learning and habit formation, encapsulated in a formula relating behavior strength to habit strength and drive. Hull later incorporated incentive motivation, recognizing both internal drives from bodily needs and the quality of external incentives. However, like preceding theories, Hull's drive theory eventually encountered criticisms for its limitations.

Incentive and arousal theories: The quest for a fourth grand theory of motivation led to exploring incentive and arousal models. Unlike drive theory, which suggests that people are pushed by needs, incentive theory argues that people are attracted to things that promise rewards and repelled by things that could lead to discomfort or harm, aiming to understand the allure of pleasure and the avoidance of pain.

Arousal theory emerged from the finding that there's an arousal center in the brain stem. It suggests that our environment influences our arousal levels: low excitement leads to boredom, the right amount triggers interest, and too much causes fear and a desire to get away. Arousal levels, therefore, guide our motivations. Though neither incentive nor arousal theories became the definitive explanation for motivation, they did advance our grasp of emotional roles, particularly in avoidance behavior.

Each of these grand theories of motivation provides a unique lens through which to view human behavior. Together, these theories form a foundational understanding of the diverse factors that influence human motivation, though they fail to offer a comprehensive understanding of what motivates humans as a whole.

Mini-Theories of Motivation

As researchers continue to seek a comprehensive theory of motivation, the focus has shifted toward examining specific elements of motivational behavior. "Mini-theories" have emerged to explain distinct facets of motivation, including individual phenomena, conditions that influence motivation, particular groups, or specific theoretical inquiries. The mini-theories include:

Self-determination theory (SDT): Focuses on the degree to which an individual's behavior is self-motivated and self-determined.

Achievement motivation theory: Examines the drive to pursue and achieve goals, emphasizing the role of aspirations and a sense of accomplishment.

Expectancy theory: Suggests that motivation is based on how much we want something and how likely we think we are to get it.

Goal-setting theory: Highlights the importance of setting specific, challenging goals in fostering motivation.

Self-efficacy theory: Centers on the belief in one's capabilities to organize and execute the courses of action required to manage prospective situations.

Intrinsic and extrinsic motivation: Differentiates between internal motivators (like personal satisfaction) and external rewards.

Abraham H. Maslow's hierarchy of needs: Proposes that people are motivated to fulfill basic needs before moving on to other, more advanced needs.

Frederick Herzberg's two-factor theory: Distinguishes between motivators (which encourage satisfaction) and hygiene factors (which can prevent dissatisfaction but don't necessarily motivate).

David McClelland's three needs theory: Focuses on three motivators that people typically have—a need for achievement, a need for affiliation, and a need for power.

Equity theory: Concerns the balance or imbalance perceived between an individual's input and output in social exchanges.

Opponent-process theory: Suggests that emotions and motivations are paired with an opposite, like fear and relief or pleasure and pain.

Each of these mini-theories offers unique insights into the factors that can drive human motivation in different contexts and are vital components of TTI Success Insights' ongoing refinement and development efforts.

SHALOM H. SCHWARTZ

As seen in the previous history of motivational theories section, the path to understanding human motivation has been complex and somewhat convoluted. To add to the confusion, a parallel line of research exploring the role of values in decision-making is intricately intertwined with human motivation and, therefore, must also be explored to understand the current theories better.

Values have been a theme in social science research since the 1800s. Much like the history of motivation, the role of values lacked any agreeable definition or any well-developed, direct ties to motivational theory literature. That changed as a result of the work of Shalom H. Schwartz.

Schwartz was a mid-20th-century psychologist who made significant contributions to the field through his research on values and motivation. After earning his master's degree in social psychology and group development from Columbia University and completing rabbinical studies, Schwartz obtained his Ph.D. from the University of Michigan. He served as a professor at the University of Wisconsin–Madison and as a visiting lecturer at the Hebrew

University. In 1979, Schwartz moved to Israel and joined the psychology department at the Hebrew University.

Schwartz's research journey started with analyzing why people help others and culminated in his detailed Schwartz Theory of Basic Human Values. He laid the groundwork through several key studies, leading to his definitive model that characterizes values by six distinctive features.

1. Values are beliefs linked inextricably to effect
2. Values refer to desirable goals that motivate action
3. Values transcend specific actions and situations
4. Values serve as standards or criteria
5. Values are ordered by importance
6. The relative importance of multiple values guides action

Schwartz's theory of motivation suggested that there are 10 universal values that drive human action. These values are self-direction, stimulation, hedonism, achievement, power, security, conformity, tradition, benevolence, and universalism. Schwartz theorized that these values are structured within a circular continuum, allowing for the examination of the dynamic interplay between conflicting and complementary values. Neighboring values on this continuum are compatible, while those positioned across from each other are often in opposition.

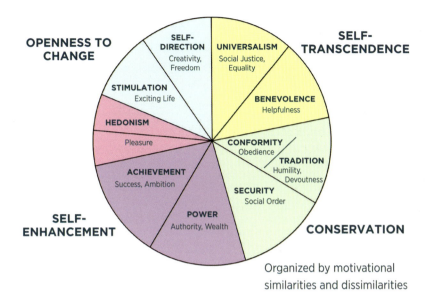

Schwartz's Concentric Model of Values diagram.[7]

This theory is instrumental in various fields, including cross-cultural psychology, as it provides a framework for understanding and comparing cultural differences and similarities in value systems. The model has been applied in numerous sociological and psychological studies, offering insights into how values influence actions and societal norms.

However, Schwartz's theory has not been without criticism. One notable point of contention is its exclusion of work-related values. Critics argue that the model does not fully consider the motivational factors specific to professional environments and occupations. Since work constitutes a significant part of life and can be a central source of identity and purpose, this omission is seen as a gap in the theory's applicability to all domains of life.

---

7. Schwartz, S.H. (1992). Universals in the Content and Structure of Values: Theoretical Advances and Empirical Tests in 20 Countries. *Advances in Experimental Social Psychology*, 25, 1–65: https://doi.org/10.1016/S0065-2601(08)60281-6

Despite these criticisms, Schwartz's Theory of Basic Human Values remains a foundational framework in the study of human motivation, offering a comprehensive system for understanding how values influence behavior and decision-making across the globe.

EDUARD SPRANGER

Eduard Spranger was a German philosopher and psychologist known for his work in human values and motivation. His influential book, *Types of Men*, published in 1914, presents his theory of personality types based on individuals' dominant value orientations. Spranger proposed six value types:

> **Theoretical**: This individual views the world with an objective lens, striving to discern its inherent order and the frameworks governing it. They pursue knowledge purely for the sake of understanding, rather than for any financial gain or practical use. Such a person is typically seen as intellectual, with a deep appreciation for learning.
>
> **Economic**: The economic individual is interested in that which is useful. Through this person's eyes, objects are evaluated for their intrinsic worth and utility from the individual's viewpoint, not the object.
>
> **Aesthetic**: Form and harmony are the desires of the aesthetic person, and this type seeks self-actualization.
>
> **Social**: The social type has a true love of people and, through love, finds power. These individuals are often viewed as being selfless.
>
> **Political**: The political attitude is characterized by a need for power.
>
> **Religious**: Unity is the value of the religious individual. This person seeks to find the highest meaning in life and to develop a system for living their life based on that highest meaning.

Spranger's theory suggested that the primary source of motivation for individuals stems from their adherence to one of these value dimensions more than the others. For example, a person with a dominant theoretical orientation would be primarily motivated by the pursuit of knowledge. In contrast, someone with a social orientation would be driven by love and compassion for others.

His ideas have had a lasting impact on the study of motivation and personality, providing a framework for understanding how individuals' values influence their actions and decisions. Spranger's concepts have been utilized in various fields, including education, career counseling, and organizational development, to help understand and guide human behavior.

THE ALLPORT-VERNON-LINDZEY ASSESSMENT

From Eduard Spranger's work, the Allport and Vernon Study of Values (SOV) was one of the earliest theoretically well-grounded questionnaires for measuring personal values. The SOV was developed by psychologists Gordon Allport, Philip E. Vernon, and Gardner Lindzey. It was first introduced in 1931 and became a significant psychological instrument used in research and practice.

The SOV categorizes values into six major types:

- **Theoretical**, which values knowledge and truth
- **Economic**, which prioritizes utility and practical affairs
- **Aesthetic**, which seeks harmony and beauty
- **Social**, which values love and altruistic behavior
- **Political**, which is concerned with power and influence
- **Religious**, which seeks unity and understanding of life's meaning

Respondents are presented with scenarios and choose between options that align with different values. The assessment then scores the relative importance of each value type to the individual based on their choices. The total score is out of 240 points, with the theoretical average for each value being 40. This helps to create a profile of an individual's value orientation, offering insights that can be applied in various contexts such as personal development, career guidance, and counseling.

BILL BONNSTETTER AND PI(A)V

It is at this point that the history of TTI Success Insights' motivation assessment finds its foundational underpinnings in the work of Eduard Spranger and other early thought leaders who applied Spranger's ideas to the professional realm with a keen focus on vocational interests.

TTI began by offering a paper-based version of the Allport-Vernon-Lindzey (SOV) assessment. The company's shift toward creating its own assessments on values and motivators started with adopting research from Russel J. Watson's studies conducted between 1983 and 1987. This research laid the foundation for TTI Success Insights' assessment called Business Values Inventory, introduced in 1988.

In 1990, Bill Bonnstetter developed the Personal Interests and Values (PIV) assessment, which gained approval for job selection within a year. Renamed Personal Interests, Attitudes, and Values™ (PIAV) by 1996, it incorporated Allport and Vernon's original constructs more closely by adding **aesthetic** and merging the **political** and **individualistic** themes. It featured 12 sections, each with six statements preceded by a contextual lead, reflecting Eduard Spranger's theory that human values are socially contextualized.

Field tests in 1996 led to renaming Spranger's **economic**, **political**, and **religious** themes to **utilitarian**, **individualistic**, and **traditional**, respectively. That year also saw the launch of a training seminar and certification process. A 2002 independent study by Peter T. Klassen confirmed the tool's reliability, which prompted updates and continuous improvements, resulting in the Motivation Insights (PIAV 2™) assessment.

The content for these assessments drew from Allport, Vernon, and Lindzey's *A Study of Values*,[8] Allport's *Pattern and Growth in Personality*,[9] and Milton Rokeach's *The Nature of Human Values*,[10] with Bill and Dr. Watson enriching the material through extensive focus group research to enhance the precision and relevance of the reports.

PIAV's Independent Evaluation

The *TTI Success Insights Motivation Insights® Technical Manual Version 1.0*[11] significantly elaborated on the initial external review of PIAV™, covering analyses of various versions of the assessment from 2003 to 2008, including international editions and validity studies. In 2014, contextual prompts were removed from the assessment to suit a global audience better, allowing for more personal interpretation. Subsequent updates in 2015 to new formatting with questions and a report were carefully vetted against foundational theories to maintain consistency with the assessment's original purpose.

---

8. Allport, G.W., P.E. Vernon, and G. Lindzey. (1960). *A Study of Values* (3rd edition revised). Boston: Houghton Mifflin.

9. Allport, G.W. (1961). *Pattern and Growth in Personality*. Holt, Reinhart & Winston.

10. Rokeach, M. (1973). *The Nature of Human Values*. Free Press.

11. Gehrig, E., Ph.D., and R. Bonnstetter, Ph.D. (2020). *TTI Success Insights Motivation Insights® Technical Manual Version 1.0*. TTI Success Insights, Ltd.: https://images.ttisi.com/wp-content/uploads/research/2020/10/21102559/PIAV2techman_2020_v1.pdf

PIAV 2 TO PME

In 2015, alongside the introduction of the 12 Driving Forces™ format, which expanded upon the original six motivators with a bidirectional perspective, the Motivation Insights assessment was updated. TTI partners were able to adopt the new Driving Forces report or continue to use the updated Motivation Insights report, now called Personal Motivation and Engagement Legacy (PME). These revisions preserved the core motivational constructs derived from Spranger's work but introduced new terminology for the attitudes. The updated instruments ask participants to rank phrases in order of resonance, setting the groundwork for both the six motivators and the 12 Driving Forces™ reports.

Motivation Assessment Today

Assessing motivation today is a critical component in various domains, including organizational development, educational settings, and personal growth. In workplaces, these assessments are instrumental for hiring, team building, employee development, and leadership training.

> **Motivation assessments help identify individuals' intrinsic and extrinsic motivators, facilitate better job-person fit, enhance job satisfaction, and optimize team dynamics.**

In education, motivation assessment tools are used to tailor teaching methods and curricula to students' motivational profiles, fostering better learning outcomes. For personal development, these tools guide individuals in understanding their drivers, setting goals, and achieving personal fulfillment.

The advancements in technology have also integrated the use of sophisticated algorithms and data analytics into motivation assessments, allowing for real-time feedback and more personalized results. Such assessments are increasingly available online, making them accessible to a wider audience. The data gathered from these assessments can also contribute to big data analytics in psychology, providing insights into broader motivation trends across different demographics.

Integrating motivation assessments into digital platforms has also facilitated their use in e-learning environments, app-based personal development programs, and online coaching services. This wide-ranging application signifies the importance of understanding motivation in enhancing performance, satisfaction, and well-being in various aspects of life.

THE SCIENCE OF MOTIVATION IN THE FUTURE

The science and understanding of motivation have evolved significantly, with contemporary researchers contributing to its development. Our work has been pivotal in applying brain imaging research to motivation assessments.

The ongoing development in the science of motivation often involves integrating findings from neuroscience to understand the biological underpinnings of motivation. Researchers at TTI Success Insights focus on how brain-based research can inform the development of more precise motivational assessments. This includes examining how different regions of the brain are activated during motivational tasks and how this correlates with behavior and decision-making.

There's also an increasing emphasis on the dynamic nature of motivation—how it changes over time and in different situations. This understanding fueled the development of more nuanced assessment tools that can capture the variability in an individual's motivational profile.

The use of technology, including machine learning and particularly artificial intelligence, is another area where motivation research is advancing. These technologies allow for the analysis of large datasets to identify patterns in motivation that were previously unrecognized. Consequently, assessments can now be personalized to an unprecedented degree, enhancing their reliability and application.

My work through TTI encompasses these advancements, contributing to more robust and practical application of motivational science in real-world settings, such as in organizational leadership, team dynamics, educational strategies, and personal development.

Overall, the science of motivation is becoming increasingly interdisciplinary, drawing from psychology, neuroscience, data science, and technology to provide a comprehensive understanding of what drives human behavior. Researchers, like our team at TTI Success Insights, are at the forefront of translating this knowledge into tools and strategies that benefit individuals and organizations alike.

WHAT YOU SHOULD KNOW ABOUT MOTIVATION
by Carissa

Understanding motivation is understanding the *why* behind the behavior. While DISC can show you how someone behaves, it's the underlying motivations that explain why they act that way. This Science of Self™ goes deeper than observable behavior, offering insights into the inner workings that drive actions. Knowing what propels a person is key in team dynamics. It enables you to assign tasks that align with each member's intrinsic motivators, fostering a team that's energized and cohesive. When everyone is engaged in roles that resonate with their core motivations, the teamwork flows smoothly, leading to a positive and productive atmosphere.

THE SCIENCE OF WORKPLACE COMPETENCIES

Your success in any job depends on the value of your contribution to the organization. Managers, mentors, and professional coaches can encourage, advise, and guide you as you grow professionally. However, the ultimate responsibility for your career development is yours and yours alone. Understanding and continuously developing these competencies, especially soft skills, is not just beneficial but essential for professional growth and leadership excellence.

The workplace competency assessment tool, through the DNA Talent™ Report or DNA Job™ Report, is designed to assist you in managing and developing your career. For many jobs, personal skills are as important as technical skills in producing superior performance. For example, it doesn't matter how well you can develop a new process for digitizing customer feedback if you can't work in a team or you have continual conflict with your manager. Personal skills are often transferable to different jobs, whereas technical skills are usually more job- or industry-specific.

This chapter details the evolution of the TTI Success Insights' competencies tool and reveals the universal recognition of these workplace competencies. Organizations around the world have created their own versions of these personal attribute skills by various names, including soft skills, personal skills, non-hard skills, dispositions, habits of mind, and many others.

> **These competencies enable individuals to navigate challenges, foster a positive work culture, and drive innovation and productivity in a rapidly evolving business environment.**

For employees, being aware of one's competencies is crucial for career development. It allows individuals to understand their strengths and recognize areas for improvement, guiding their learning and development journey. Employees who excel in soft skills can collaborate effectively with diverse teams, adapt to changing circumstances, and communicate their ideas and feedback constructively. These skills are often transferable across different roles and industries, making them invaluable for career mobility and stability.

Leadership, in particular, demands a high level of competency in soft skills. A leader's ability to inspire, motivate, and guide teams hinges on their emotional intelligence, communication skills, and adaptability. Leaders who understand and harness these competencies can create a vision, navigate complexities, and foster an environment where creativity and productivity flourish. They are better equipped to handle conflicts, build strong relationships, and guide their teams toward achieving organizational objectives.

Furthermore, the importance of continually acquiring and refining these soft skills cannot be overstated. In an ever-changing business world, the capacity to learn and adapt is a competency in itself. Continuous learning not only keeps one's skills relevant but also demonstrates a commitment to personal and professional growth. This learning can take various forms, from formal education and training to experiential learning and self-reflection.

Workplace competencies are the bedrock upon which successful careers and effective leadership are built. It is a continuous journey of learning and growth, one that not only enhances individual performance but also contributes significantly to the success and resilience of the organization as a whole. In this context, pursuing these competencies becomes not just a professional obligation but a strategic imperative for lasting success and fulfillment in one's career.

EXAMPLE OF DNA FINDINGS AND IMPLICATIONS

Over the past decade, a growing number of PhD dissertation research studies have used TTI assessment tools. An example is Dr. Sandra L. Dietrich's *Critical Examination of the Construct Validity of the TTI Performance DNA™ Survey for the Purpose of Differentiating the Entrepreneurially-Minded Engineer.*[12]

Her study summary states:

> "The use of the TTI Performance DNA™ survey is helping define the vision of the next generation engineer by using analytical results to help participating universities measure program effectiveness. This research reveals that there is a difference between practicing engineers and engineering leadership in terms of professional skills; therefore, a specific profile can be established for these two groups."

---

12. Dietrich, S.L. (2012). *A Critical Examination of the Construct Validity of the TTI Performance DNA™ Survey for the Purpose of Differentiating the Entrepreneurially-Minded Engineer* (doctoral dissertation). Eastern Michigan University, Ypsilanti, Michigan.

Dr. Dietrich goes on to share that the TTI Success Insights' Performance DNA™ survey is particularly useful for universities that want to see how effective their engineering programs are.

The research from this survey has shown that there's a noticeable difference between the skills of everyday working engineers and those in engineering leadership roles. Because of this difference, we can create distinct profiles for these two groups.

For example, a typical engineering management executive (EME) is likely to show strong leadership qualities, be good at managing conflicts and setting goals, be effective in presenting and persuading others, have skills in developing employees, be creative and innovative, and be capable in personal effectiveness, management, decision-making, and self-management. However, they might not be as strong in customer service skills. Their behavior is often characterized through DISC assessments as being very driven (direct) but not as consistent or predictable (dynamic).

Additionally, there are some skills that are almost (but not quite) as strongly associated with EMEs as the ones mentioned above. These include flexibility, thinking about the future, solving problems, and negotiating effectively. For instance, when discussing flexibility, we're about 95% sure that this skill is significantly different between regular engineers and EMEs. This means we are very confident (but not 100%) that flexibility is a more notable trait in EMEs than in standard engineering roles.

In summary, this survey helps to pinpoint what makes an EME different in terms of skills and behavior, which can guide how universities shape their engineering programs and what skills they emphasize for students who aspire to be in engineering management.

HISTORY OF UNDERSTANDING WORKPLACE COMPETENCIES

Understanding the history of workplace competencies and the development of their assessment is crucial for comprehending the evolving nature of the workforce and the workplace. Initially, the focus in most organizations was predominantly on technical skills and qualifications. However, as the business environment became more complex and interconnected, there was a growing recognition of the importance of broader skill sets, including interpersonal and cognitive abilities. This shift was partly influenced by the rise of service-oriented industries—like banks, law firms, plumbing repair companies, motion picture theaters, and management consulting firms—and the increasing value placed on customer relations and teamwork. The historical evolution from a narrow focus on hard skills to a more holistic view that includes soft skills illustrates a significant change in understanding what makes an employee effective. It also reflects the changing nature of work itself, which has become more collaborative and less predictable, requiring a diverse range of skills to navigate.

Assessment methods for these competencies have also evolved. Traditional assessments, often focused solely on technical abilities or academic achievements, have gradually given way to more comprehensive methods. These include behavioral interviews, psychometric tests, 360-degree feedback (feedback from multiple people in various different areas), and performance appraisals that evaluate an individual's ability in areas like communication, leadership, problem-solving, and adaptability.

Understanding the development of these competency assessment tools is important for both employers and employees. For employers, it provides insights into how to effectively identify and cultivate the right talent for their organizational needs. For employees, awareness of these assessment methods is crucial for personal development, enabling them to align their skills with the expectations of the modern workplace. Moreover, recognizing the historical context and the evolution of these assessments helps us appreciate the broader shifts in workplace dynamics and prepares individuals and organizations for future trends in competency development.

STANFORD RESEARCH INSTITUTE AND THE CARNEGIE MELLON FOUNDATION STUDIES

The Stanford Research Institute (SRI) International, along with the Carnegie Mellon Foundation, have conducted various studies that have been instrumental in shaping our understanding of workplace competencies, particularly the role of soft skills. In the 1960s and 1970s, these studies began to highlight that professional success was not determined by technical skills and knowledge alone. The groundbreaking research by SRI, often cited alongside contributions from the Carnegie Foundation for the Advancement of Teaching, pointed out that up to 75% of long-term job success depended on soft skills, while only 25% was attributed to technical knowledge.[13]

These findings were revolutionary at the time and have had a lasting impact on how employers and educators view employee training and development. The studies conducted by these institutions identified

---

13. According to the Carnegie Foundation for the Advancement of Teaching, these statistics were extrapolated from *A Study of Engineering Education*, authored by Charles Riborg Mann and published in 1918 by the Carnegie Foundation. The cited figures come from the data on pages 106-107. The report is out of print and may be available through a public or university library, however a digital reproduction may be accessible through one of the following links: https://www.nationalsoftskills.org/downloads/Mann-1918-Study_of_Engineering_Educ.pdf; https://archive.org/stream/studyofengineeri00mannuoft/studyofengineeri00mannuoft_djvu.txt

a range of nontechnical skills that were critical for effective job performance. These included problem-solving, the ability to work in a team, communication skills, and self-management. These competencies have been found to be crucial across industries and positions, from entry level to leadership roles.

The research undertaken by SRI and supported by insights from the Carnegie Foundation laid the groundwork for the modern competency frameworks that many organizations use today. These frameworks not only guide hiring and promotion decisions but also inform the design of training programs aimed at developing these key skills in the workforce. The emphasis on soft skills has also influenced educational policies, with a push toward incorporating these competencies into curricula from an early age.

The legacy of these studies is evident in the ongoing dialogue about the importance of soft skills in the 21st-century workplace. As automation and artificial intelligence change the nature of many jobs, the uniquely human skills that cannot be replicated by machines become even more valuable. The foresight of SRI and the Carnegie Foundation in recognizing the importance of these skills has ensured that soft skills remain at the forefront of discussions about workforce preparedness and the future of work.

OTHER UNIVERSITY STUDIES

University studies across the globe have also significantly contributed to our understanding of workplace competencies beyond technical expertise. For instance, research from Harvard University has echoed the sentiment that soft skills such as communication, empathy, and adaptability are paramount for professional success.[14] Similarly, MIT's Sloan School of Management has explored how leadership and collaboration are critical for innovation in the workplace.

The University of Michigan's Ross School of Business has conducted studies emphasizing the need for cultural competency in an increasingly globalized business environment. These competencies are seen as vital for navigating cross-cultural communication and for managing diverse teams.[15]

In the U.K., the University of Cambridge has explored the correlation between soft skills and job performance, suggesting a strong link between an individual's soft skill set and their ability to perform in complex and dynamic work environments.

Collectively, these studies underscore a shift in the understanding of what attributes contribute to individual and organizational success. They advocate for a balanced skill set that includes both technical knowledge and a range of interpersonal and strategic competencies. This body of research has been influential in shaping recruitment, training, and development strategies in modern organizations, highlighting the ongoing need for investment in soft skills development.

TTI SUCCESS INSIGHTS' ALIGNMENT WITH EDUCATIONAL AND WORKPLACE STANDARDS

Recognizing the importance of soft skills in the workplace is one thing, but accurately assessing them is another due to the lack of

---

14. Deming, D.J. (2016). *The Growing Importance of Social Skills in the Labor Market.* Harvard University and NBER (National Bureau of Economic Research): https://economics.harvard.edu/files/economics/files/deming_socialskills_noappendix_aug2016_seminar-12-9-16_0.pdf

15. Deepa, S., and M. Seth. (2013). Do Soft Skills Matter? Implications for Educators Based on Recruiters? Perspective. *The IUP Journal of Soft Skills*, 7(1):7–20.

THE SCIENCE OF WORKPLACE COMPETENCIES

a universally accepted definition or theory. The concept of competence is diverse in its interpretation, with numerous definitions existing within the social sciences. Yet, the approach to competence we took at TTI is gaining international traction for its solid theoretical foundation.

TTI has approached the definition of competence with a blend of scientific credibility and practical relevance, placing an emphasis on the skills that are crucial in the workplace.

The release of "Education for Life and Work: Developing Transferable Knowledge and Skills in the 21st Century" by the National Research Council provided a benchmark for us to evaluate the DNA 23™ skills, ensuring they were aligned with national educational priorities. This report also offered a robust conceptual framework, placing the assessment within a well-articulated theoretical backdrop.[16]

The National Research Council categorizes workplace competencies into three main areas: cognitive, intrapersonal, and interpersonal. Cognitive competencies include skills related to thinking, such as problem-solving and memory. Intrapersonal competencies are about self-management, controlling one's behaviors and emotions to achieve goals. Lastly, interpersonal competencies involve communication skills—how ideas are expressed to others and how people understand and respond to the messages they receive.

Cognitive skills or abilities are the different ways a person's brain handles tasks like remembering information, paying attention, reasoning, understanding language, and solving problems. They are

---

16. Pellegrino, J.W., and M.L. Hilton, editors. (2012). "Education for Life and Work: Developing Transferable Knowledge and Skills in the 21st Century," National Research Council: https://nap.nationalacademies.org/catalog/13398/education-for-life-and-work-developing-transferable-knowledge-and-skills

essential for processing and organizing new information. When a person learns something new, these skills help to organize this information in their brain for future use. And when the time comes to recall this information, it's their cognitive skills that retrieve it for use. Improving these skills can make this whole process more efficient and make sure new information is properly grasped and applied.

In a work setting, cognitive abilities allow people to make sense of complex data, keep the company's objectives in mind, stay focused during critical meetings, and remember relevant past details. These abilities enable people to link what they've learned before with new information, which can make them more productive and effective in their roles.

Key workplace cognitive skills include the ability to analyze information, make decisions, think critically, learn and adapt to changes, organize and plan (often referred to as executive function), solve problems, listen actively, interpret various forms of communication, innovate, reason, debate, understand and use technology, and think creatively.

Intrapersonal abilities cover a broad spectrum of skills and attributes that relate to an individual's internal understanding and management of themselves. This includes adaptability to changing situations, upholding integrity, valuing diversity, and having a keen interest and curiosity in intellectual matters. It involves self-awareness and self-regulation, a commitment to ongoing learning, and an appreciation for the arts and culture.

Self-evaluation and taking initiative are also key components of intrapersonal skills, along with maintaining productivity, upholding professional and ethical standards, and being flexible. The domain extends to metacognition, which is thinking about one's thinking process, self-direction in managing one's learning and goals, and maintaining both physical and mental health.

Grit and a strong work ethic, along with conscientiousness, are crucial for resilience and perseverance in the face of challenges. Citizenship skills reflect a sense of responsibility and participation in the community. The intrapersonal domain also includes self-reinforcement, which is the ability to motivate oneself, persist in pursuing goals, take responsibility for one's actions, and orient oneself toward a career path.

The **interpersonal** skills domain encompasses a wide range of abilities crucial for effective interaction and collaboration with others. These skills include effective communication, influencing social dynamics positively, taking responsibility, communicating assertively, and demonstrating leadership qualities. They also involve reasoning and making persuasive arguments, showing empathy and understanding others' perspectives, building trust, and possessing various competencies for interacting well with others.

These skills cover how a person presents themselves in a professional setting, coordinates activities, adopts a service-oriented attitude, engages in negotiation, resolves conflicts, and collaborates effectively. Interpersonal skills are essential for fostering teamwork and cooperation, ensuring that individuals can work together harmoniously and productively.

BILL BONNSTETTER AND TTI SUCCESS INSIGHTS' DNA 23™ ASSESSMENT

In 1998, Bill embarked on a research project to identify what was then known as personal skills. His investigation found that only one system, used by major corporations, was in place to identify these skills. The system listed 67 individual skills. However, closer scrutiny of this system revealed several issues: many of the skills were vaguely defined, there were unclear links to their practical application in the workplace, and evaluating all 67 skills posed a significant challenge. With these insights, Bill began to conduct his own research and develop a strong, reliable workplace competency framework for assessments.

A year later, TTI conducted pivotal work on workplace competencies that has had a lasting impact on how businesses understand and leverage human potential.

TTI's research focused on identifying the key competencies that are most predictive of success in the workplace. The competencies assessment was built upon the premise that while traditional hiring often overemphasizes education, experience, and skills, it is the underlying behaviors, motivators, and personal skills—collectively known as soft skills—that are the true determinants of job performance and satisfaction.

The TTI assessment identified 23 key personal skills that were categorized into three main areas:

- Personal skills
- Interpersonal skills
- Business skills

Personal skills included goal orientation and personal accountability, which reflect an individual's drive and self-reliance. Interpersonal skills encompassed diplomacy and empathy, which are crucial for teamwork and customer service. Business skills highlighted leadership and project management, both important for organizational success.

This was initiated by Bill in 1999 through interviews with key TTI associates who brought expertise in essential workplace people skills. This led to the development and copyright of TTI's first workplace competency assessment tool, known as DNA 23™, in 2000.

THE SCIENCE OF WORKPLACE COMPETENCIES

TTI also emphasized the importance of applying this understanding to employee development and coaching. Rather than using assessments for selection purposes only, TTI advocated for their use in developing current employees. By recognizing individual strengths and areas for improvement, organizations could better align their workforce with company goals and support employee growth.

The research work that led to DNA 23™ also underlined the adaptability of workplace competencies across various job levels and industries. Bill believed that while the relative importance of each competency might vary by role or sector, the overall framework was universal. This made the TTI assessment tools highly versatile and valuable for a broad range of clients.

The findings of TTI contributed to a growing body of evidence that soft skills are critical for effective job performance. These competencies are less about what individuals know and more about how they apply their knowledge in various situations. This insight was particularly prescient considering the rapid technological changes and globalization affecting the labor market.

Bill's work with TTI extended beyond the assessment to include developing educational materials and training programs that helped organizations implement competency-based HR practices. TTI's tools have been used for employee selection, onboarding, team-building, and leadership development, demonstrating the broad applicability of their research.

The DNA 23™ assessment of workplace competencies marked a significant advancement in the field of human resources and organizational development. By creating a comprehensive framework to assess and develop the whole person, DNA 23™ has helped countless organizations optimize their human capital. TTI's tools and methodologies continue to shape the way companies think about talent, potential, and performance in the workplace.

Following the introduction of new national guidelines, there was a reassessment and expansion of the original set of 23 competencies in DNA 23™, which led to the addition of two more, bringing the total to 25 in 2013. Later, in 2017, based on input received from TTI's extensive network, five of the existing constructs were substituted, and their working definitions were further refined. This process resulted in an updated list, again comprising 25 distinct workplace competencies.

TTI is dedicated to continuous improvement and as part of this commitment, our research team has developed a series of guidelines for creating and reviewing our assessments regularly. An important part of these guidelines is the requirement that every assessment is based on a strong theoretical foundation. To achieve this, TTI has published a competencies technical manual containing the research and findings TTI conducted along with an extensive global literature review to document a world-wide perspective on workplace competencies.[17] This method keeps TTI Success Insights leading in offering cutting-edge and frequently updated assessment tools.

THE PROCESS FROM THEORY TO APPLICATION

From the beginning, to create and test an accurate way to assess workplace competencies, TTI planned on a three-step system:

- Define the competencies
- Create interview questions for each skill to be used in the assessment

---

17. Gehrig, E., Ph.D., and R. Bonnstetter, Ph.D. (2021). *TTI Success Insights Workplace Competencies Technical Manual Version 1.0.* TTI Success Insights, Ltd.: https://ttiresearch.com/project/workplace-competencies-technical-manual-version-1-0/

- Develop 360-degree feedback surveys for each skill to verify the accuracy of the assessment

Defining the competencies was challenging because there was no agreement in the literature as to what those should be. Our initial job assessment checked for five key personal skills, which we later increased to seven. In other words, what are the top seven personal skills, that belong to one of the three defined categories of skills, required for successful job performance?

Interview questions were created for each skill to build the assessment, which was designed to evaluate people's job-related abilities. People identified as being excellent at certain personal skills were interviewed to make sure they actually had the skills they claimed to have.

The question-creation process led to the development of a full set of 360-degree feedback questions, which were used later to double-check the accuracy of the personal skills assessment,

After getting the assessment results, 360-degree surveys were conducted. This provided three types of evidence: the assessments, named DNA Talent™ (which measures the individual's skills) and DNA Job™ (which measures the skills that lead to superior performance in the job); the personal interviews that provided confirmation with evidence; and the cross-checking from five different people who answered the 360-degree surveys.

This method was used for all 25 personal skills in the DNA competencies assessment. Each skill was confirmed through interviews with seven people, 10 times each, making it 70 confirmations per skill. For the 360-degree feedback, we needed at least four out of five people to agree that the person had the skill.

Checks were also done on people who were experts in more than one skill. Confirmation was limited to a maximum of five personal skills per person, so the number of questions in the 360-degree survey was capped at five for each skill, for a total of 25 questions.

These original personal skill models were then compared and correlated against new emerging National Research Council (NRC) publications and international soft skill recommendations. The following table shows how the TTI competency assessments correlation compared to the NRC domains.

NRC Domain	DNA 25™ (2013)	DNA 25™ (2017)
Cognitive Domain	Creativity & Innovation Conceptual Thinking Decision-Making Futuristic Thinking Planning & Organizing Problem Solving Ability	Creativity & Innovation Conceptual Thinking Decision-Making Futuristic Thinking Planning & Organizing Problem Solving Time & Priority Management
Intrapersonal Domain	Continuous Learning Flexibility Goal Achievement Personal Accountability Resiliency Self-Management	Continuous Learning Flexibility Goal Orientation Personal Accountability Resiliency Self-Starting
Interpersonal Domain	Conflict Management Customer Focus Diplomacy & Tact Employee Development/ Coaching Empathy Interpersonal Skills Leadership Negotiation Persuasion Presenting Teamwork Understanding & Evaluating Others Written Communication	Appreciating Others Conflict Management Customer Focus Diplomacy Employee Development/ Coaching Influencing Others Interpersonal Skills Leadership Negotiation Project Management Teamwork Understanding Others

CHALLENGES

Defining workplace competencies is much more complex than identifying traditional skills like math or specific product knowledge. There's no clear consensus on what to even call these "non-hard skills," with terms like soft skills, interpersonal skills, and many others used. Despite over a century of literature highlighting their importance in work and life, many organizations and educational institutions haven't fully recognized or effectively assessed these skills. TTI Success Insights has addressed these challenges as we built and continue to improve our workplace competency assessment tool.

There's no universally agreed-upon list of competencies, with reviews identifying over 100 potential competencies. Often, the rationale for including or excluding certain skills is not clearly defined. Furthermore, many competencies are specific to certain contexts and change with evolving job expectations, which means assessments need to be flexible and prioritized accordingly.

Different organizations may agree on a competency but define it in varied ways. Additionally, many competencies are interrelated or form subsets of larger categories. For instance, critical thinking might include creativity, and effective communication could encompass a range of sub-skills like cultural awareness and listening.

Various methods are used to measure these competencies, including self-reports, 360-degree feedback, standardized tests, and direct observation. Each method needs solid justification and evidence of reliability. Self-report assessments can be unreliable, as studies show that most people overestimate their performance. TTI addresses these biases with brain imaging and continuous monitoring to ensure accuracy.

Lastly, while experience is key to developing most competencies, it's recognized that some skills are harder to develop this way or are more inherent to individuals. This understanding requires precise differentiation between skills and inherent dispositions.

THE DNA WORKPLACE COMPETENCIES ASSESSMENT TODAY

We have gone to great lengths to describe how TTI Success Insights has created and tested workplace competencies assessments. Even though the original one was created almost 25 years ago, the solid theoretical foundation it was created upon and the review and testing that we have continued to do has created an assessment that stands up to time and scrutiny. Now more than ever, employees and leaders need to understand and grow these essential soft skills.

THE SCIENCE OF WORKPLACE COMPETENCIES IN THE FUTURE

Scientists and researchers in the field of workplace competency assessments face numerous challenges due to rapidly evolving work environments, technological advancements, and changing societal norms. One of the primary challenges is keeping pace with technological change, as the skills relevant today may quickly become outdated. Additionally, the increasing globalization and cultural diversity of the workforce present the challenge of integrating cultural differences into competency assessments.

Measuring soft skills like emotional intelligence and adaptability, which are less tangible than technical skills, poses another significant challenge. Predicting the competencies needed for future jobs, especially in emerging fields, requires forward-thinking and adaptable research methodologies. Moreover, with the rise of big data and artificial intelligence (AI) in assessments, addressing data privacy and ethical considerations has become crucial. Balancing the need for standardized assessments that are universally applicable while also being customizable to specific organizational contexts adds to the complexity.

Looking ahead, employees will likely need to develop competencies in new areas:

- Digital literacy to stay proficient in new technologies
- Emotional and cultural intelligence for working in increasingly diverse environments
- Critical thinking and problem-solving skills for navigating information overload
- Adaptability and flexibility for coping with rapid changes
- Sustainable and ethical decision-making skills, as sustainability becomes more central to business operations

TTI Success Insights is committed to addressing these evolving challenges. Our commitment is demonstrated through continuous research and development to refine our assessment tools, ensuring global and cultural inclusivity in our assessments, embracing technological advancements like AI and machine learning to enhance accuracy and reliability, adhering to strict data privacy policies and ethical standards, designing tools that are adaptable to different organizational needs, and providing training and education to ensure effective and ethical implementation of our assessments. This ongoing dedication places us at the forefront of developing sophisticated, culturally informed assessment tools essential for the modern workforce.

WHAT YOU SHOULD KNOW ABOUT WORKPLACE COMPETENCIES
by Carissa

Knowing your competencies can be extremely impactful when positioning yourself for success in the workplace. When you're aware of what you excel at most, you can present yourself effectively to hiring committees and showcase your best skills that fill their needs. Or you can use them to start conversations with your current supervisor to exemplify the responsibilities you can take on or the roles you can fill, based on your strengths. While it's common to fixate on areas of weakness and it's beneficial to bolster those areas, prioritizing your strengths is key—they're your greatest assets. Recognizing what you're good at helps you find the right fit for your skills, shaping not just the role you choose but also the type of work environment where you'll thrive.

THE SCIENCE OF EMOTIONAL INTELLIGENCE

Emotional intelligence (EI), also known as emotional quotient (EQ), can best be described as the ability to monitor one's own and other people's emotions, to discern between different emotions and label them appropriately, and to use emotional information to guide thinking and behavior.

Emotional intelligence involves four main skills: self-awareness, self-management, social awareness, and relationship management. Self-awareness is about recognizing your own emotions and understanding their impact on your thoughts and actions. Self-management refers to controlling impulsive feelings and behaviors, handling emotions in a healthy way, and adapting to changing situations. Social awareness deals with empathy—understanding others' emotions, needs, and concerns and being comfortable in social settings. Relationship management is about the ability to build and maintain good relationships, communicate effectively, inspire and influence others, collaborate in a team, and handle conflicts.

> **Emotional intelligence plays a crucial role in both work and personal life.**

People with high EI/EQ are often more adaptable, resilient, and successful in their relationships. They are skilled communicators, leading to better teamwork and a more positive work environment.

Emotional intelligence also continues to be an essential component in determining leadership effectiveness, especially when leaders are dealing with teams in the workplace. Research suggests that successful leaders and superior performers have well-developed emotional intelligence skills.[18] This makes it possible for them to work well with a wide variety of people and to respond effectively to the rapidly changing conditions in the business world. In fact, a person's emotional intelligence may be a better predictor of successful performance than traditional cognitive intelligence (IQ).

Emotional intelligence is also linked to mental well-being. It's associated with handling stress better, feeling more satisfied at work, and having stronger personal relationships. Basically, while a high IQ might help you land a job, a high EI/EQ is what helps you excel and find fulfillment in that job.

THE TRANSFORMATIVE EFFECTS OF UNDERSTANDING YOUR EQ

Angie Lion, a TTI Success Insights partner, shared with me recently about how understanding and growing her emotional intelligence changed her life.

> "Developing emotional intelligence is one of the most impactful skills anyone can cultivate to enrich their personal and professional life. It's a skill set that can be enhanced with willingness

---

18. Srivastava, K. (2013). Emotional intelligence and organizational effectiveness. *Industrial Psychiatry Journal*, 22(2), 97–99: https://www.ncbi.nlm.nih.gov/pmc/articles/PMC4085815/

and effort, leading to transformative changes in how one perceives the world and navigates relationships.

"As someone who wasn't raised in an environment with a high level of emotional intelligence, this skill was a game changer for me personally and professionally. I am highly committed to continuous improvement in this area of my life. Over the past eight years, I have coached and trained individuals from a variety of backgrounds: students, people coming out of incarceration, executives, business owners, and elected officials. Again and again, I hear testimony that these skills are not only life changing but even life saving. People often wonder why no one taught them this earlier in life. In school, we are taught the 'three Rs,' and we give no attention to understanding ourselves or others. We aren't offered the tools we need for the most important journey we have (our lives).

"In my own experience of life, I was fascinated by the human body and how it worked. I became a surgical technologist so I could assist in surgeries. As the years went on, working in the OR (operating room), I became fascinated by how the leaders (the surgeons) and the emotions that they brought into the room impacted the team both positively and negatively. I watched how each person handled those interactions differently. When I became an instructor of surgical technology, I was taking a college course where I read Daniel Goleman's book and wrote a paper on EQ and how it has impacted my life. That was the beginning of my commitment to growing my emotional intelligence and surrounding myself with people who would help me accomplish this.

"In 2016 I met Ron Price, and I went through The Complete Leader Program. I was introduced to the five sciences of self at that time, but EQ was the one I dove straight to the deep end with. I recognized how my upbringing (being raised by a teenage single mother and experiencing 8 out of the 10 identified adverse childhood experiences)[19] impacted how I experienced the world and the people in it. My awareness grew, and soon I was better able to regulate my own emotions as well as separate myself from 'catching' other people's moods. I became certified in EQ, and I have been growing my skills and helping others to grow these essential human skills ever since.

"Some call these abilities 'soft skills,' but nothing is soft about them. If anything, they are the 'hard skills' that require continuous learning and improvement, which is a journey that never ends. We can improve until we take our last breath.

"I am committed to helping people who want to understand themselves and others better. I see growing EQ as a direct line to enhancing our life experience.

"All it takes to grow these skills is a little curiosity, humility, and a willingness to become a lifelong learner."

THE HISTORY OF EMOTIONAL INTELLIGENCE

It is important to not only understand how EQ plays a role in our work and relationships, but also the history of the concept and how it has been researched, expanded, and refined. Understanding the history of emotional intelligence provides context for how the

---

19. Adverse childhood experiences (ACEs) are potentially traumatic events that occur from ages 0-17 years. See https://www.cdc.gov/violenceprevention/aces/fastfact.html

concept has evolved over time from being a peripheral idea in psychology to a widely recognized and important aspect of personal and professional development.

Tracing the development of EQ shows how the understanding of EQ has deepened and become more nuanced. This historical perspective also helps us appreciate the interdisciplinary roots of EQ, drawing from areas such as psychology, neuroscience, and education, which enriches our understanding of the concept. More detail on the history of EQ as well as the research and validation for TTI's Emotional Quotient assessment and the EQ Talent Report are included in the *TTI Success Insights Emotional Quotient 2019 Technical Manual Version 1.2*.[20]

Edward Thorndike

Edward Lee Thorndike, a prominent American psychologist in the early 20th century, played a foundational role in developing the concept of emotional intelligence, though the term itself was not coined during his time. Thorndike, renowned for his work in educational psychology and the theory of learning, introduced the idea of "social intelligence" in 1920, which laid the groundwork for what would later evolve into the concept of emotional intelligence.

Thorndike defined social intelligence as the ability to understand and manage people, to act wisely in human relations. This was a significant departure from the prevailing views of intelligence at the time, primarily focused on academic and logical reasoning abilities. Thorndike's recognition of social intelligence as a distinct form of

---

20. Gehrig, E., Ph.D., and R. Bonnstetter, Ph.D. (2022). TTI Success Insights Emotional Quotient 2019 Technical Manual Version 1.2. TTI Success Insights, Ltd.: https://images.ttisi.com/wp-content/uploads/research/2022/06/23085423/EQtechman_2020_v1.2_June_2022.pdf

intelligence marked the first step toward acknowledging that cognitive intelligence (IQ) wasn't the only important factor in determining a person's ability to succeed in life.

His early understanding emphasized that human intelligence was multifaceted and that success in social and emotional domains was just as crucial as traditional academic skills. Thorndike's perspective highlighted the importance of interpersonal skills, empathy, and the ability to navigate social situations—elements that are central to modern conceptions of emotional intelligence.

Although Thorndike's work in this area was not extensively developed during his lifetime, his ideas were instrumental in shaping subsequent theories of emotional intelligence. His recognition of the importance of social and emotional competencies paved the way for later psychologists to explore and expand upon these ideas, leading to the comprehensive framework of emotional intelligence as we understand it today.

Mowrer's Understanding of the Importance of Emotions

O. Hobart Mowrer, a well-known psychologist from the mid-20th century, was another influencer who greatly impacted how we understand emotional intelligence. Even though Mowrer, like Thorndike, didn't come up with the emotional intelligence term, his research and ideas have been important in shaping our understanding of how emotions affect our behavior and mental health.

Mowrer is famous for his learning theory, which focuses on the importance of emotions in learning. He believed that emotions aren't just side effects of learning; they're actually a central part of it. Mowrer thought that how we respond emotionally helps us understand how we learn from what happens around us, particularly when it comes to the consequences of what we do. This is important for emotional intelligence because it shows how key it is to be aware of and manage our emotions when we're learning and making decisions.

In his work on therapy and mental health, Mowrer stressed how crucial it was to be honest about our emotions. He advocated for recognizing and expressing even negative emotions, challenging the idea that we should hide or ignore these feelings. This belief is central to emotional intelligence, which is about knowing, understanding, and expressing our emotions in an appropriate way.

Mowrer also examined how emotions are important in developing our morals and ethics. He suggested that emotions have a large role in shaping our sense of right and wrong and how we make moral decisions. This ties in with emotional intelligence skills like empathy, awareness of others' feelings, and managing relationships, where understanding and responding to other people's emotions is crucial.

Overall, Mowrer's work helped lay the foundation for understanding how important it is to be aware of and control our emotions. This is essential for growing as a person, getting along with others, and staying mentally healthy. All of these are key parts of emotional intelligence.

> " . . . emotions are of quite extraordinary importance in the total economy of living organisms and do not deserve being put into opposition with 'intelligence.' The emotions are, it seems, themselves a higher order of intelligence."
>
> —O. Hobart Mowrer

Payne and Bar-On

Wayne Payne and Reuven Bar-On were two of the significant contributors to the field of emotional intelligence in its early development. Each offered unique insights that have greatly influenced how we understand and apply this concept today.

Wayne Payne is particularly noted for being one of the pioneers in the field of EQ. In 1985, he wrote a doctoral thesis titled *A Study of Emotion: Developing Emotional Intelligence*, one of the earliest known academic works to use the term "emotional intelligence" specifically. Payne's research focused on the importance of emotions in our lives and proposed the concept of emotional intelligence as a key factor in managing our emotional well-being. His work laid an early foundation for future research on EQ, highlighting the significance of acknowledging, understanding, and regulating emotions.

Reuven Bar-On made a major impact through developing a model and an assessment tool for emotional intelligence. His Bar-On model suggested that emotional intelligence involves various emotional and social skills that help us handle life's demands and pressures. He created one of the first tools to measure EQ, known as the Emotional Quotient Inventory (EQ-i), which evaluates several emotional and social skills, such as self-awareness, empathy, handling stress, and interacting with others.

Bar-On's work has been particularly influential in showing how emotional intelligence can be applied in real-life situations, such as the workplace or schools. His model indicates that EQ is crucial for success in many areas of life, going beyond the traditional idea of intelligence as just cognitive ability.

Together, Payne and Bar-On have expanded our understanding of emotional intelligence. Payne's early exploration introduced the term into the academic world, while Bar-On's practical model and tools have helped bring EQ into everyday use. Their work collectively highlighted the importance of emotional and social skills in achieving personal and professional success, establishing EQ as an essential field of study in psychology and human development.

The Bar-On Model

The Bar-On model, developed by psychologist Reuven Bar-On, is a comprehensive framework for understanding and assessing emotional intelligence (EQ). This model plays a pivotal role in the field of EQ, offering a multifaceted approach to measuring emotional and social competencies.

According to the Bar-On model, emotional intelligence encompasses a variety of skills and characteristics that impact a person's ability to cope with environmental demands and pressures. Bar-On described EQ as:

" . . . an array of non-cognitive capabilities, competencies, and skills that influence one's ability to succeed in coping with environmental demands and pressures."[21]

The model identifies five key areas of EQ:

> **Intrapersonal skills**: This involves self-awareness and self-expression. It includes understanding one's own emotions, recognizing personal strengths and weaknesses, and expressing one's feelings and thoughts nondestructively.

---

21. Bar-On, R. (1996). *The Emotional Quotient Inventory (EQ-i): A Test of Emotional Intelligence.* Toronto, Ontario: Multi-Health Systems.

Interpersonal skills: These skills are about the ability to develop and maintain relationships, empathize with others, and recognize and understand the emotions of other people.

Adaptability: This includes flexibility in handling change, solving problems, and coping with novel situations.

Stress management: This area focuses on managing stress and controlling impulses. It involves being resilient and maintaining control under pressure.

General mood: This encompasses the overall outlook on life and includes aspects such as optimism and happiness.

Bar-On's model is unique because it views emotional intelligence as a set of skills that can be improved with practice rather than fixed traits. It's been influential in both personal development and organizational contexts, helping individuals enhance their EQ for better personal well-being and professional success. The Bar-On model has also led to the development of practical assessment tools, like the Emotional Quotient Inventory (EQ-i), widely used for evaluating EQ in various settings.

Salovey and Mayer

In 1990, Peter Salovey and John D. Mayer, renowned American psychologists, proposed a formal definition and framework for emotional intelligence that significantly influenced the field of psychology. Their groundbreaking work laid the foundation for understanding EQ as a distinct form of intelligence, separate from traditional cognitive abilities measured by IQ.

Salovey and Mayer defined emotional intelligence as "the ability to monitor one's own and others' feelings and emotions, to discriminate among them, and to use this information to guide one's thinking and actions."[22]

Their model highlighted four key components of EQ:

- Reflective regulation of emotions
- Understanding and analyzing emotions
- Emotional facilitation thinking
- Perception, appraisal, and expression of emotion

The Mayer-Salovey Model was initially known as the Four Branch Model of Emotional Intelligence.

Salovey and Mayer's framework proposed that emotional intelligence is a form of social intelligence that involves the ability to monitor emotions—both one's own and those of others—and to use this information to guide one's actions and thinking. Their model provided a scientific basis for understanding emotional intelligence, distinguishing it from general intelligence, and laid the groundwork for further research and development in this field.

The Mayer-Salovey Model of emotional intelligence was informed by a broad spectrum of contemporary theoretical research from other influential psychologists. In 1997, Salovey, along with collaborator Sluyter, unveiled a four-dimensional model that has since underpinned many modern assessments of EQ, framing it as a collection of measurable abilities.[23]

---

22. Salovey, P., and J.D. Mayer, (1990). Emotional intelligence. *Imagination, Cognition, and Personality*, 9(3), 185-211. SAGE Publications.
23. Salovey, P., and D.J. Sluyter, (1997). *Emotional Development and Emotional Intelligence: Educational Implications.* New York: Basic Books, a Division of Harper-Collins Publishers.

Salovey believed it is important to do more than just identify an individual's EQ. He believed that it may be improved through training and development programs. Hence, it is possible for one's EQ to change throughout one's life. This view is held by others, including Bar-On and Mayer.

Their work on emotional intelligence has been fundamental in shaping how people think about and use this concept today. Their ideas have impacted how businesses and organizations understand their employees' behavior and how individuals work on their own personal growth. The research done by Salovey and Mayer on emotional intelligence has helped change the way we look at emotions and how they affect our work and personal lives.

Daniel Goleman

Daniel Goleman was a science writer for *The New York Times* for more than 12 years, specializing in brain and human behavior research. He studied psychology at Harvard University, where he worked with David McClelland and others. Goleman was introduced to the work of Salovey and Mayer during the 1990s, which led to the publication of two books by Goleman: *Emotional Intelligence* and *Working with Emotional Intelligence*.[24]

While Salovey and Mayer laid the theoretical foundation for emotional intelligence, Goleman is credited for popularizing the concept with his marketing flair and prolific writing abilities. He introduced EQ to a wider audience with the premise that emotional intelligence is a key factor in determining success in life. He argued that it is even more important than cognitive intelligence (IQ). Goleman's

---

24. Goleman, D. (2006). *Emotional Intelligence: Why It Can Matter More Than IQ*. Bantam; Goleman, D. (1998). *Working with Emotional Intelligence*. Bantam.

interpretation of EQ included a range of skills and characteristics such as self-awareness, self-regulation, motivation, empathy, and social skills.

One of Goleman's significant contributions was highlighting the application of EQ in various life domains, particularly in the workplace. He argued that emotional intelligence is critical for effective leadership, teamwork, and interpersonal relations in professional settings. This perspective led to the development of training programs and workshops aimed at enhancing EQ skills in corporate environments.

Goleman's model of EQ consists of five main domains:

- Self-awareness
- Self-regulation
- Internal motivation
- Empathy
- Social skills

Beyond his book *Emotional Intelligence*, Goleman's numerous articles, talks, and subsequent books have continued to influence the understanding of emotional intelligence. He has contributed to expanding the research on EQ, emphasizing its importance in diverse areas such as education, leadership, and personal development.

Goleman's work has been foundational in making emotional intelligence a topic of global discussion. He has helped bridge the gap between academic research and practical application, making the concept of emotional intelligence accessible and relevant to a broad audience. His influence has been instrumental in cementing the importance of emotional and social competencies in personal and professional success.

Over time, the notion that emotional intelligence accounts for 80% of life's success has taken root, though Daniel Goleman himself never made this claim. People have eagerly embraced this idea as part of a formula for success. The concept spread rapidly through mainstream media, raising expectations for improved personal and professional outcomes. Yet, even after more than 20 years, definitive evidence to substantiate these claims is still being sought.

EMOTIONAL INTELLIGENCE CURRENT ASSESSMENTS

Like the other sciences of self, measuring EQ using self-reported questionnaires is a widely used method that relies on individuals assessing their emotional intelligence. These questionnaires typically consist of a series of statements or questions about the respondent's feelings, behaviors, and attitudes in various situations. The respondents are asked to rate each item based on their experiences and perceptions.

The TTI Success Insights Emotional Quotient™ report, originally based on Goleman's EQ model, is a specialized tool that delves into the intricacies of an individual's emotional intelligence. We define EQ as the capacity to recognize, comprehend, and effectively harness one's emotions to promote increased collaboration and productivity. This concept is crucial in today's dynamic work environments, as it directly impacts interpersonal relations and professional effectiveness. The TTI EQ™ report is structured to offer insights into two principal domains: **self** and **others**, each encompassing critical aspects of emotional intelligence.

In the self domain, the report focuses on these aspects:

Self-awareness: This is the foundational aspect of emotional intelligence. It involves an individual's ability to accurately perceive their emotions and understand their impact on their behavior and mindset. High self-awareness enables people to recognize how their feelings affect their interactions and decision-making processes.

Self-regulation: A subset of self-management, self-regulation refers to the ability to control or redirect disruptive emotions and impulses. It involves staying in control under stress or challenges, and displaying adaptability and resilience.

Motivation: The inner drive that propels individuals toward their goals, characterized by a persistent passion and energy for achievement and improvement. It is essential for maintaining effort through challenges, pivotal for personal fulfillment, and critical for success in professional endeavors.

In the others domain, the report explores these aspects:

Social awareness: This component relates to understanding others' emotions, needs, and concerns. It encompasses empathy and the ability to pick up on emotional cues of others, fostering an environment of trust and respect in interpersonal interactions.

Social regulation: Building on social awareness, this skill involves the aptitude to develop and maintain good relationships, communicate effectively, inspire and influence others, work well in a team, and manage conflict. It's about leveraging emotional intelligence to improve and strengthen connections with others.

By evaluating these areas, the TTI Success Insights EQ™ report provides a comprehensive overview of how an individual's emotional intelligence influences their interactions and effectiveness in both personal and professional spheres. Understanding and developing these facets of emotional intelligence can lead to better teamwork, leadership, and overall success in various aspects of life.

The results offer valuable insights into the respondent's emotional strengths and areas for improvement. This can guide personal development, therapy, or professional growth activities focused on enhancing emotional skills.

Setting the Standard

Numerous evaluations sprang up from psychologists' research into EQ. Still, early critiques from experts raised issues about bias, the actual validity of what was being measured, and other factors that determine an assessment's legitimacy. These critiques didn't write off these tools as ineffective; rather, they highlighted a need for more stringent design standards and comprehensive research to back up their efficacy.

In response to those early critiques, TTI Success Insights placed a high priority on refining EQ assessments to meet stringent standards. TTI's approach is rooted in rigorous research and an unwavering commitment to scientific validation, ensuring that their Emotional Quotient assessments are not only unbiased and precise but also relevant and applicable in a variety of professional settings. This dedication to quality underpins the development of TTI's EQ tools, embodying the industry's leading practices for measuring emotional intelligence. Through continuous innovation and validation studies, TTI aims to provide assessments that are not just reflective of an individual's emotional competencies but are also instrumental in guiding their personal development and professional growth.

EQ AT WORK

Dr. Laura Shero's dissertation studied the possible impact of our recent pandemic on EQ.[25] She provided background for her study with these statements:

> "Emotional intelligence (EI) has been established as a critical skill with the ability to influence positive outcomes and mitigate challenging situations. Research connects EI to such benefits as better health, superior job performance, and psychological well-being.
>
> "This study provides important evidence of the stability of EQ/EI during highly stressful and chaotic circumstances."

While her study did not find significant EQ/EI changes in the general population, she does offer a rationale as well as a key finding associated with a sub-population:

> "The negative impact of the COVID-19 pandemic on mental health is well documented (Killgore et al., 2020[26]; Wang et al., 2020[27]). Therefore, a word about the relationship between EI and mental health, and what our results do and do not mean regarding mental health, is appropriate. EI is not a measure of depression, anxiety, or stress. EI is a measure of how readily a person recognizes their depression, anxiety, and stress (among

---

25. Shero, L.R. (2023). *Examining the Stability of Emotional Intelligence Among U.S. Adults Before and After the Onset of the COVID-19 Pandemic*. Baylor University, Dissertations Publishing. 30574555.

26. Kilgore, W.D.S., E.C. Taylor, S.A. Cloonan, and N.S. Dailey. (2020). Psychological resilience during the COVID-19 lockdown. *Psychiatry Research*, September, 191, 113216: https://www.ncbi.nlm.nih.gov/pmc/articles/PMC7280133/

27. Wang, C., R. Pa, X. Wan, Y. Tan, L. Xu, R.S. McIntyre, F.N. Choo, R. Ho, V.K. Sharma, and C. Ho. (2020). A longitudinal study on the mental health of general population during the COVID-19 epidemic in China. *Brain Behavior, and Immunity*, 87 (July 2020), 40-48: https://www.sciencedirect.com/science/article/pii/S0889159120305110

other emotions) and to what degree they have tools to regulate these emotions. But EI is not a measure of these states. Therefore, research demonstrating that EI remained stable does not contradict research showing that the U.S. experienced a mental health crisis in relationship to COVID-19. In fact, to some degree, high levels of EI can contribute to heightened awareness of negative emotions."

However, when she examined the literature of the sub-population with occupations associated directly with the medical field, she discovered a decrease in empathy and overall EI/EQ scores due to the COVID-19 pandemic. The literature suggested that prolonged stress and exposure to human suffering were the mechanisms for decreased EQ among both medical students and practitioners across a range of medical professions.

Another noteworthy finding was found in our own EQ technical report. After several years of collecting demographics, including the age of EQ reporters, no significant difference in EQ assessment scores has been found related to age.[28] This directly contradicts the "belief" that EQ improves with age. The new data suggested that the old belief was more wishful thinking than factual.

THE SCIENCE OF EQ IN THE FUTURE

Today, emotional intelligence is recognized for its role in enhancing communication, empathy, and conflict resolution skills. Organizations increasingly value EQ for leadership development,

---

28. Unpublished report contained within the TTI Emotional Quotient Technical Manual: Gehrig, E., Ph.D., and R. Bonnstetter, Ph.D. (2022). TTI Success Insights Emotional Quotient 2019 Technical Manual Version 1.2. TTI Success Insights, Ltd.: https://images.ttisi.com/wp-content/uploads/research/2022/06/23085423/EQtechman_2020_v1.2_June_2022.pdf

team building, and talent acquisition, and they are incorporating EQ training into their professional development programs. Moreover, educational curricula integrate EQ concepts to foster social and emotional learning among students.

Looking to the future, EQ is poised to become even more integral to our professional and personal lives. As artificial intelligence and automation advance, the uniquely human skills encapsulated by EQ—such as empathy, creativity, and interpersonal relationships—are expected to be in higher demand. The future of EQ science also points toward more sophisticated assessments that can better measure and track emotional competencies over time, using technology like biometrics and machine learning to provide deeper insights.

Furthermore, the burgeoning field of neuroleadership, which merges neuroscience with management techniques, underscores the potential of emotional intelligence to enhance decision-making and leadership. As we understand more about the brain's emotional mechanisms, EQ training could become more personalized, with interventions tailored to individual neurological profiles.

In essence, the trajectory of EQ science is one of greater integration into various aspects of life. Its applications may expand into improving mental health, enhancing educational outcomes, and even informing public policy. With ongoing research underscoring its importance, EQ stands to redefine what it means to be "intelligent" in the 21st century.

EQ'S FUTURE ASSESSMENTS

As we look to the future of emotional intelligence as a science, it is poised for an era of remarkable growth and innovation. The burgeoning interest in EQ, driven by its proven impact on personal and professional success, sets the stage for deeper scientific exploration. We can anticipate advancements in neuroscience and psychology to offer more nuanced insights into how emotional intelligence functions within the brain. These insights will likely challenge and expand our current understanding, potentially leading to new sub-domains within the field of EQ. Moreover, integrating artificial intelligence and machine learning in psychological research promises to uncover patterns and correlations previously hidden in vast datasets. This will not only refine existing EQ models but also enable the development of more sophisticated frameworks that account for cultural, environmental, and biological factors. In addition, TTI Success Insights unique multi-science approach will open new insights into the interrelationships between EQ, behavioral styles, motivations, competencies, and acumen capacities.

In terms of practical applications, the future promises a range of innovative tools and techniques to enhance EQ. We will likely see the rise of personalized EQ training programs, which can adapt to individual learning styles and emotional profiles. These programs will offer more effective and engaging ways to develop emotional intelligence skills, from empathy and self-awareness to emotion regulation and social skills. Wearable technology and mobile applications are expected to play a significant role, providing real-time feedback and situational prompts to help individuals practice and improve their EQ in everyday life. As we move forward, the fusion of technology, science, and personalized learning will open new horizons in understanding and enhancing emotional intelligence, making it an even more integral part of our personal and professional lives.

The history of emotional intelligence is marked by the significant contributions of theorists and practitioners who have deepened our understanding of human emotions. The models developed by Salovey, Mayer, Goleman, and others have been instrumental in shaping EQ, turning what were once considered mere soft skills into well-defined competencies. As we adapt to this constantly changing environment, the knowledge we've gained from EQ will be invaluable in helping us fully utilize our emotional capabilities, leading to more fulfilling and interconnected lives. The journey of EQ is ongoing, and it will continue to evolve, driven by the experiences and research of those who engage with it daily.

WHAT YOU SHOULD KNOW ABOUT EMOTIONAL INTELLIGENCE
by Carissa

Emotional Intelligence (EQ) starts with a deep knowing of your emotions and your behaviors that then spring from those feelings. It's about understanding your own experience, and recognizing in real time the impact it will have on yourself internally, as well as on those around you. Regulating yourself can prove to be difficult in heightened emotional states, but with practice, it can be a powerful skill. EQ becomes crucial when handling difficult relationships, whether in your personal life or at work. Challenges and conflicts can stir strong emotions, and it's easy to react in the moment—often in ways we might later regret.

Committing to mutual respect and being mindful of your influence is vital for life success. People with high EQ create a sense of safety, allowing open communication even during disagreements. Essentially, EQ is the subtle yet powerful fabric that holds workplace interactions together, ensuring a cohesive environment.

THE SCIENCE OF THE HARTMAN VALUE PROFILE

The Hartman Value Profile (HVP) is an innovative psychological assessment tool designed to offer profound insights into an individual's value system and decision-making processes. Developed by Dr. Robert S. Hartman, the founder of formal axiology, the HVP is based on the principle that how we value and interpret our experiences fundamentally shapes our perceptions, actions, and choices. This tool provides a structured method to understand these often subconscious valuation processes, allowing for a deeper understanding of oneself.

WHAT IS AXIOLOGY?

According to Merriam-Webster, axiology is "the study of the nature, types, and criteria of values and value judgments especially in ethics."

At its core, the HVP measures an individual's capacity to make value judgments across three distinct dimensions:

- Systemic
- Extrinsic
- Intrinsic

The **systemic** dimension assesses how a person values organization, structure, and consistency, often reflecting their approach to rules and logical systems. The **extrinsic** dimension focuses on the practical aspects of life, such as task completion and the external attributes of people and things. In contrast, the **intrinsic** dimension delves into the inherent worth and uniqueness of oneself and others, revealing a person's capacity for empathy and understanding of human nature.

By evaluating these dimensions, the Hartman Value Profile offers a multifaceted view of an individual's thinking patterns and priorities. It can uncover how personal biases and value assessments influence decision-making and interpersonal relationships. This insight is particularly valuable in personal development, as it can highlight areas of strength and potential growth. For instance, a high intrinsic score might suggest strong empathetic abilities, while a lower systemic score could indicate a more flexible approach to rules and structures.

In practical terms, the TTI HVP assessment, called the Acumen Capacity Index (ACI) report, can be a transformative tool for self-awareness and personal development. It helps individuals understand their unique perspective on the world, guiding them in aligning their actions with their core values. This alignment is crucial for personal satisfaction, effective decision-making, and building meaningful relationships.

In a broader sense, the Hartman Value Profile serves not just as a mirror reflecting one's current value system but also as a map guiding toward a more self-aware and fulfilling life.

UNDERSTANDING YOUR WORLDVIEW

Ron Price, current President of TTI Success Insights, is an expert in the Hartman Value Profile and has seen that assessing your HVP with the Acumen Capacity Index (ACI) report can lead to a greater understanding of how you see the world around you (**worldview**) and yourself (**self-view**). Ron summarized his thoughts about the HVP:

> "I was introduced to formal axiology at a TTI Success Insights conference in 2004. I was immediately intrigued and began an exploration into the Hartman Value Profile and how understanding how you see the world and how you see yourself in the world can lead to transformations, both personally and professionally. Through providing assessments to others and helping them understand themselves, I have seen positive change in people's lives."

Ron related the following true stories (names have been changed) from his coaching experiences that show how the ACI assessment has greatly impacted individuals by helping them understanding their worldviews and self-views:

> "Tim, an engineer in the tech industry, aimed to enhance his empathy toward others. This was a goal highlighted in his ACI report. To achieve this, Tim focused on becoming more aware of his biases in evaluating people. He undertook an exercise designed to expand his ability to appreciate individual differences. Tim conducted 30-minute interviews with three people who differed significantly from him: one with opposing political views, another from a distinct religious background, and a third from a vastly different economic situation. This effort to understand rather than judge or 'fix' these individuals broadened his empathy. As a result, Tim's improved interpersonal skills led to a promotion into a leadership role—a position he likely wouldn't have secured otherwise.

"Maria discovered her tendency to micromanage, recognizing her excessive focus on her team's details. This newfound self-awareness led her to embrace delegation, allowing her to grant her team more autonomy and focus on their development. As a result, she assumed larger roles within her organization and gained recognition as a thought leader. Similarly, another leader we coached realized his habit of overcommitting. He found that while each individual task seemed manageable, the cumulative effect of his constant agreement made his workload unmanageable.

"Shauna, through coaching, uncovered a deep-seated trust issue with authority figures. This realization enabled her to enhance her communication with her supervisor, fostering a more cooperative work environment. As a result, she earned greater independence and respect in her role.

"Carl, like many others we've worked with, was struggling with self-doubt instilled by early criticism from figures like parents or teachers. We've also seen cases where a strong attachment to past successes caused a kind of self-centeredness that blocked personal development. After addressing these issues, Carl and others were able to look forward to new chances for growth with fresh excitement without disregarding the value of their previous experiences or achievements.

"This evaluation helps people understand how well they are engaging with their roles, whether at work or in their personal lives. It often sparks crucial discussions. For example, Juan, after reviewing his assessment, understood that his job wasn't fulfilling and decided to pursue a career change. On the flip side, we've also seen individuals like Juan who work excessively, finding too much satisfaction in their job, which can negatively impact their personal life and health.

"We worked with Dan, a person brimming with optimism but unclear about his career direction. In exploring his assessment, it became evident that Dan's uncertainty was due to an overwhelming number of positive opportunities. He needed a clear method to sift through these options and select the ones that would best help him achieve his long-term goals.

"The ACI assessment, based on the Hartman Value Profile, has prompted hundreds of conversations that enlightened me and the people I coached. Over time, the framework of this report has come to influence everything I do, making me a better person in the process."

ROBERT S. HARTMAN, THE FATHER OF "FORMAL AXIOLOGY"

Robert S. Hartman was born Robert Shirokauer on January 27, 1910, in Berlin. In his autobiography, *Freedom to Live: The Robert Hartman Story*, Robert attached significance to the fact that he was born across the street from the Ministry of War on the emperor's birthday.[29]

As a young child, he witnessed the bewildering loyalty to the emperor that made death a celebrated expression of patriotism during WWI. Later in grammar school, one of his teachers had the students recite this quote every day at the beginning of class, "I was born to die for Germany." In his formative years, this preoccupation with "legitimate killing" troubled Hartman deeply. It set the stage

---

29. Hartman, R., and A. Ellis. (2013). *Freedom to Live: The Robert Hartman Story*, Second Edition. Wipf and Stock Publishers, Eugene, Oregon.

for a lifelong quest to understand how otherwise intelligent people would proudly embrace the taking of human life as an expression of love for their country.

Initially, Hartman pursued a law degree, expecting to find answers to this dilemma. Unfortunately, it was during his years in law school and his early years serving as an assistant district judge in Berlin that Hitler and the Third Reich came into power. Incredulously, Hartman concluded that Chancellor Hitler "had the law on his side." This made it abundantly clear to Hartman that knowledge, wisdom, and good judgment would not come through a study of the law. Good people may use the law for good purposes, but clearly bad people would also use the law for bad purposes. He concluded the law was, in and of itself, only an amoral tool—neither good nor bad.

Hartman's outspoken criticisms of Hitler resulted in the need to leave Germany in 1932, using a false passport. The gift of this false passport led him to legally change his name to Robert S. Hartman. Initially, he found his skills in photography earned him enough money in Paris to avoid starvation. Photography also took him to England, where he photographed the historical first launch of a rocket by German scientist Gerhard Zucker. Eventually, Hartman put his law degree to good use by convincing Walt Disney to designate him as the representative of Disney's intellectual property in Scandinavia, with its headquarters in Copenhagen. It was during this time in Scandinavia that he met and married his wife, Rita Emanuel Hartman. When WWII became inevitable, Walt Disney agreed to allow Hartman to represent the company in Latin America. Hartman's communication skills in German, French, Swedish, English, and Spanish, as well as his growing judgment capacities, made him a trusted advisor and administrator for the company.

THE SCIENCE OF THE HARTMAN VALUE PROFILE

What Is Good?

In 1941, Hartman and his wife migrated to the United States, where he earned his Ph.D. in philosophy at Northwestern University. The focus of his doctoral dissertation was the question, "Can field theory be applied to ethics?"[30] It was during these years that Hartman began to form his deep desire to answer an age-old question of philosophers: "What is good?"

In Plato's *Republic*,[31] there is a famous passage:

> Glaucon says to Socrates, "*How, old man, you have talked about the problem aplenty—tell us the solution.*"
>
> Socrates replies, "*My dear Glacon, the solution does not belong in this dialogue. For those, we have to have another dialogue. I can't tell you what goodness is; I can only tell you what it is like. It is like the sun that radiates everything, that warms everything, that makes everything fertile and brings forth everything.*"

Another way to describe Plato's conundrum may be to answer the question, "What is it that a good home, a good daughter, a good cheese, and a good holiday all have in common?"

Over the centuries, philosophers would take up the question without a satisfactory conclusion. In 1903, British philosopher George E. Moore published *Principia Ethica*,[32] attempting to establish a logical parallel to the contributions made by Sir Isaac Newton in his book *Mathematical Principles of Natural Philosophy*.[33] Moore wrote,

---

30. https://www.hartmaninstitute.org/life-of-robert-s-hartman

31. Plato. (1943). *Plato's The Republic*. Books, Inc., New York.

32. Moore, G.E. (2004 reprint). *Principia Ethica*. Dover Publications; 1st edition.

33. Newton, Sir Isaac, I.B. Cohen (translator), A. Whitman (translator), and J. Budenz (translator). (2016). *The Principia: The Authoritative Translation and Guide: Mathematical Principles of Natural Philosophy* (First Edition). University of California Press.

"I know that goodness is but not *what* it is." Though he tried and failed for decades to answer the question "What is good?" he did advance the quest by concluding in 1922 that "good is not a descriptive property." A modern way to explain this statement is that if I send you an invitation to visit my house by simply directing you to my street and then saying, "Mine is the good house." it will be of little use to you.

Hartman was haunted by this question, "What is goodness?" and even his doctoral dissertation proved unsatisfactory. As he wrote years later, "My dissertation had been all wrong. I had committed the naturalistic fallacy by confusing goodness itself with a thing that was good, namely, the potentiality of a situation. The nature of goodness itself could only be approached, I decided, through the nature of the word, 'good.'" He spent years thinking about the word *good*, making note of its uses and definitions. He collected thousands of samples of the word in use and spent his sabbatical year in 1949 trying to wring the answer from his piles of evidence.[34]

It was on Christmas Eve, 1949, while he was putting some books away in his home library, that he had the epiphany that would set the course for the rest of his academic and professional life. After decades of wrestling with the question, the answer dawned on him in an instant.

> **Hartman wrote in his journal, "A thing is good when it has all of the properties associated with its concept."**

---

34. From Hartman's *Freedom to Live: The Robert Hartman Story*, pages 32-35.

This meant that the common denominator between a good house, a good meal, a good car, a good spouse, and a good criminal was the extent to which each of these fulfilled their concept, or in other words, the extent to which they included the properties of their definition.

To most, this may have seemed an overly simple and insignificant discovery. But for Hartman, it set the stage for a life of impact, joy-filled learning, and international distinction. Though he didn't invent the term "formal axiology," he gave it substance and practical application. The term was originally penned by Edmund Husserl but without any further explanation.

Hartman became a highly respected academician in the company of many other great thinkers of his time, including Abraham Maslow, Viktor Frankel, Gordon Allport, and others. He taught at Ohio State University, MIT, and Yale University and eventually became the Chair of Excellence in the Department of Philosophy at the University of Tennessee. His work in formal and applied axiology also led to significant contributions in business, including the founding of the Council of Profit Sharing Industries in the U.S., which eventually led to the U.S. practice of funding employee 401(k) retirement programs. Hartman also completed significant consulting assignments with companies like Sears Roebuck & Company, Nationwide Insurance, and Alcoa Aluminum.

Formal Axiology—the Study of Value

In Hartman's writing, formal axiology is described as the capacity to recognize meaning or value in any object. He later broke possible objects into three categories: ideas (he referred to ideas as systemic value), things (extrinsic value), and people (intrinsic value). From this initial insight, Hartman and others eventually developed the rudimentary framework of logic that they hoped would revolutionize the social sciences in the same way that mathematics had revolutionized the natural sciences.

Some records indicate that mathematics has a 5000-year head start and just as Galileo (1564-1642) and others struggled with academic acceptance of their work, Hartman struggled with winning over other philosophers—many of whom resented the idea of moving axiology out of the field of philosophy into a new science of value.

Because of the close relationship between philosophy and psychology, Hartman began experimenting with a self-administered assessment in 1960. His objective was to see whether he could measure an individual's judgment or patterns of attaching value or meaning to various objects:

1. Ideas
2. Things
3. People

This eventually became known as the Hartman Value Profile, and it is the basis on which the Acumen Capacities Index was designed at TTI Success Insights. Over the last 70 years, variations on this assessment have been used in the fields of psychology, business management, personnel management, economics, sociology, hiring, professional growth, etc.

Part of the catalyst for Hartman's development of the Hartman Value Profile was inspired by a seminar conducted by Professor Eric Fromm's class in psychoanalysis. Dr. Hartman also interacted extensively with Dr. Viktor Frankel, founder of logotherapy, author of *Man's Search For Meaning*, and Dr. Abraham Maslow, the creator of

Maslow's Hierarchy of Value. Robert Hartman was nominated for the Nobel Peace Prize in 1973, shortly before he died.

> **Hartman referred to this new assessment as "an X-ray of the soul," and in another instance, he referred to it as "a psychosocial X-ray."**

He vehemently objected to his assessment being called a personality or psychometric assessment, insisting that it measured a person's instinctual judgment or valuing patterns and, as such, it reflected a much deeper reflection of a person's identity.

The HVP assessment is made up of two lists of 18 items that are placed in a predetermined order for the respondent to reorganize based on a specific set of instructions. The first list of 18 items, intended to measure a person's worldview, is to be organized from the most value, or good, to the least value, or worst. The second list of 18 items, intended to reveal a person's self-view, is to be organized from the statement the individual agrees with the most in the number 1 slot to the statement the individual agrees with the least in the number 18 slot.

Hartman was vehement that this assessment was not a personality assessment but rather a way to better understand how an individual attaches meaning and as a result, makes decisions both in interpreting the external world of ideas, things, and people, and the internal world of being, doing, and thinking. The statements used in the assessment have evolved as society and language have changed, but the basic logic structure Hartman created has stood the test of time.

Other Contributors to the Study of Axiology

There have been many axiologists who have contributed to our understanding and application of formal axiology. However, David and Vera Mefford have probably played the most significant role in our learning and subsequent applications of this logic structure for the social sciences.

David Mefford was an undergraduate student of Robert Hartman at the University of Tennessee. Their friendship grew, and when David Mefford moved to Europe to complete his master's degree at the University of Heidelberg, he also served as Robert Hartman's European business representative. While there, David worked with Siemens, Volkswagen, and the Siebert Institute using Hartman's theories and methods to enhance organizational development and leadership strategies. His work primarily focused on applying axiological principles to improve corporate decision-making and ethical practices. David also met Vera in 1974 while completing his studies in Europe. After returning to the United States, David earned his doctorate in philosophy at the University of Tennessee and co-founded The Hartman Institute with John Davis in 1977, five years after Robert Hartman's death.[35]

In memorializing David, who passed away on April 30, 2014, the Hartman Institute wrote this statement:

"David was a pioneer in the true sense of the word, a creative genius who witnessed and helped a new science emerge by fully developing a universal model and methodology for a scientific frame of reference for practical applications of Axiology."

---

35. https://www.hartmaninstitute.org/index.php?option=com_dailyplanetblog&view=entry&year=2021&month=04&day=08&id=17:hartman-history-series-david-mefford

In addition to advising TTI Success Insights in product development, David and Vera trained many members of the TTI Success Insights community in the practical applications of formal axiology.

TTI'S AXIOLOGY ASSESSMENTS

The earliest version of the Hartman Value profile was incorporated into TTI's library of assessments in 2003. This was called the Attitude Index™, and it was licensed from a Hartman Value Profile provider. In early 2006, this report was replaced by the Personal Talents, Skills, and Insights Report™ (PTSI™), co-developed by David & Vera Mefford and staff at TTI Success Insights. This version provided an expanded report that included the Dimensional Balance Page. This was the first ever visualization of clarity and bias for the three worldview dimensions (Empathetic Outlook, Practical Thinking, Systems Judgment) and the three self-view dimensions (Sense of Self, Role Awareness, Self-Direction). The PTSI™ report included the original scoring methodology of Hartman plus several interpretive scores formulated by the Meffords in collaboration with TTI Success Insights.

The next iteration of the Hartman Value Profile, the Acumen Capacities Index Report™, was introduced in 2012. This report holds more closely to the scoring and descriptions found in Hartman's *Manual of Interpretation*. Though the scoring remains the same as found in Hartman's work, many of the descriptions have been modernized in order to enhance understanding by coaches and respondents.

The Hartman Value Profile has been utilized and adapted by many axiologists over more than 50 years, with millions of respondents completing various assessments based on the axiological logic structure Hartman created.

Hartman died suddenly and unexpectedly of a heart attack on September 20, 1973, but not before inspiring many of his students to carry on his quest. Today, the Hartman Institute at the University of Tennessee houses his archives and regularly gathers axiologists from around the world to build on his work. Numerous papers, research studies, and books have been written to advance Hartman's work.

> ### RULES OF FORMAL AXIOLOGY
>
> The academic language associated with formal axiology has been one of the challenges in popularizing formal axiology and its many practical applications. To overcome this barrier, TTI has "translated" much of the academic language into 15 "rules" of formal axiology. This is a work in progress to be tested, debated, and improved for many years to come. The rules of formal axiology are as follows:
>
> **1. A thing is good when it fulfills its concept.** This means that a bicycle is good when it fulfills our concept of a bicycle. When we imagine a bicycle, what do we see in our mind? Two wheels or tires? A seat? Handlebars? A bicycle is then good if it has these components. Hartman would say, "The bicycle fulfills its definition."
>
> **2. There are three dimensions of value:**
>
>   a. People (intrinsic)
>
>   b. Things (extrinsic)
>
>   c. Ideas (systemic)
>
> **3. There are three ways to define value:**
>
>   a. Absolutely (all or nothing, yes or no)

THE SCIENCE OF THE HARTMAN VALUE PROFILE

    b. Comparatively (poor, fair, average, good, excellent)

    c. Uniquely (one-of-a-kind)

Hartman described the absolute way of defining value as systemic. An example of this is categorizing a thing as a building or a tree. It is absolute. Comparatively, or as Hartman described it, extrinsically, we can define a house or tree further by identifying the features that make it different from other houses or other trees. Examples would be a house with two stories versus one. We could also define a house as a new house versus an old house or an expensive house versus an inexpensive house. There are some comparisons that will identify a house as poor, fair, average, good, or excellent in a way that virtually all people will agree with, but there are other ways of comparing houses that would be more dependent on specific needs or preferences. Finally, to recognize a house as unique or one-of-a-kind, or as Hartman would have described as the intrinsic definition of a house, we would recognize that this house may have been custom-designed by a famous architect, such as Frank Lloyd Wright. This intrinsic definition of the house is another definition of value, regardless of whether we like or dislike the house, which is described better in rule 5.

4. In understanding any person, thing, or idea, the definitions are integrated with each other. The intrinsic always contains the extrinsic, and the extrinsic always contains the systemic. This means that when we are looking at a Frank Lloyd Wright-designed house (intrinsic), it also has contained within its definition a series of tangible features that can be used to compare it against other houses, and that systemically or absolutely, it is fundamentally, a house.

5. The hierarchy of value is that ideas are good, the practical is better, and total fulfillment is best. To stay with the example of a house, fulfilling the systemic definition of being a house is good, the additional features of the house represent more or better value, and when this house is also one-of-a-kind is best. In concept, Hartman believed that the systemic (idea of a house) is good, the extrinsic (tangible realities) of the house are better, and the intrinsic (unique attributes of the house) are best. This can also be applied to recognizing the value potential in an idea is good, the value potential in a tangible thing is better, and the value potential of a person is best. This is axiologically true, but there can be other factors that are more difficult to apply.

6. Valuation can be described as our relationship or preferences toward objects (people, things, ideas). This rule acknowledges that an object, either a person, thing, or idea, has value in and of itself, but its value to us may be different based on our needs or preferences. This introduces the role of bias, another word for preference or opinion. For instance, a Tesla has value potential in and of itself, but two people can have very different opinions about the same Tesla based on their needs and preferences—their biases. The same valuation of making an object better or worse than it is can hold true for any idea, any tangible thing, or any person.

7. The relationship between logic and emotion helps us understand how we valuate—whether positively, negatively, or with objective neutrality. Though logic and emotion are intertwined in our brains, we can learn to separate objective facts about an object from our needs, preferences, or emotions toward the same object. We can value one sports team above another because of our preference (loyalties), or we can also disvalue a sports team because we don't like them for one or more reasons. "Like," "Love," or "Hate" all represent an emotional aspect of valuation. It is also possible to have a neutral valuation of a sports team, neither preferring nor disliking them, but only thinking of them objectively. Often, we are not immediately aware of the significance of emotions in the formation of our opinions. This can result in being overly accepting or overly critical in our valuations.

8. We can apply bias in all three dimensions. In other words, we can overvalue or undervalue ideas absolutely, comparatively, or uniquely. Likewise, we can also overvalue or undervalue things or persons absolutely, comparatively, or uniquely. To overvalue or undervalue absolutely (systemically), we could say, "I love all cats!" or, "I hate all cats!" To overvalue or undervalue comparatively (extrinsically), we could say, "I like calico cats, but I don't like black cats." To overvalue or undervalue uniquely (intrinsically), we could say, "I had a very special relationship with that cat," or "I never liked that cat!"

9. Valuation depth or intensity grows along a continuum from systemic to extrinsic to intrinsic.[36] Because systemic value is good, extrinsic value has more goodness potential, and intrinsic has the greatest goodness potential (see rule 5), the intensity of our overvaluation or undervaluation will tend to intensify along the continuum, reaching its highest intensity

---

36. Edwards, R.B. (2010). *The Essentials of Formal Axiology*. University Press of America.

in the intrinsic dimension. As an example, when thinking of a house, a person will normally have less emotion than when comparing one house with another. Their greatest emotional response will come from identifying a unique, one-of-a-kind house. The same can be true when thinking about an idea systemically, extrinsically, or intrinsically and can also be true when thinking about a person along this continuum.

10. The higher the clarity scores, the more significant subtle differences in valuation will be. This may be the most difficult rule to understand. It states that on a scale of 1–100, the differences between a score of 90 or 95 are more significant in making value judgments than the differences between a score of 40 and 50. Using the Richter Scale as an analogy can help illustrate this concept. Think of the scale measuring the energy release of earthquakes: small increments at higher magnitudes signify vast differences in energy. For instance, the jump from 6.0 to 6.1 on the Richter Scale indicates a significant increase in energy release, much more than the jump from 4.0 to 4.1.

11. We grow our clarity of the world or self from the systemic to the extrinsic to the intrinsic (knowing, doing, being). In most cases, we develop our understanding of an idea, a thing, or a person from the basic concept to the comparative properties, then to the unique attributes. In self-development, we grow most effectively by first defining the ideal skill or concept of ourselves, then beginning to practice with a focus on the ideal skill or concept of ourselves, then finally, by achieving the ideal skill or concept of ourselves through eventual mastery.

12. Value can be explored and created more deeply by applying the model of fractals of Systemic, Extrinsic, and Intrinsic. As an example, we can define or create value by looking at the subsets of an idea—a systemic object—systemically, extrinsically, and intrinsically. Deeper levels of understanding and value creation continue as we move deeper using the same fractal model with ideas, things, or people. This opens up the possibilities of a pathway of continuous value creation without knowing what our limits are in the depth or richness of value creation.

13. An axiology virtuoso has learned to see and act in a balanced way across all three dimensions. A virtuoso has practiced and mastered defining, developing, and mastering practical axiology instinctively with ideas, things, and people. In this same way, this person is able to define, practice, and become the best version of himself continually with a seeming infinity of potential (though probably not literally).

14. There is a phenomenology of axiological patterns of value. Just as the periodic table accelerated the discovery of chemical elements, a "periodic table" of formal axiology might dramatically accelerate the advancement of the social sciences. This was explored by David Mefford in his doctoral dissertation, *Phenomenology of Man as a Valuing Subject*, and his subsequent practice as an axiologist.

15. When we value an object intrinsically over time, we identify with it so closely that we can "become one" with it. Stated differently, we are not ourselves without it. This can be true for a person, a thing, or an idea. For example, consider a family home that has been cherished for generations. Its significance

> transcends its market value or physical features, symbolizing heritage, childhood memories, and a deep sense of belonging. For the individuals in this family, the house is not just a building but a vital part of their identity and personal narrative. According to Hartman's concept, their profound connection with the home has evolved to the point where their sense of self and the house have become intrinsically intertwined.

HARTMAN VALUE PROFILE TODAY

Modern neuroscience has opened significant insights into the reasons why the Hartman Value Profile and Acumen Capacities Index™ assessments are so useful in understanding an individual's tendencies in making judgments. Neuroscientists believe, and TTI has been able to prove through EEG-measured responses, that at least 95% of judgments begin in the pre-cognitive activity of the brain. With deliberate and intentional processing, we can either validate or invalidate the initial responses in the prefrontal cortex of the brain, but this means the vast majority of judgments and decisions made by humans are subject to precognitive processing. Our brain science experiments have proven this to be true.[37]

TTI Success Insights' Earliest Brain Activity Response Processing Efforts

Our initial attempt to link brain activity with participant responses began with an experiment where we collected electroencephalograms (EEGs) from participants as they were shown each of the 18 items from the Hartman assessment in a random order. The results

---

37. See www.ttiresearch.com

of this first experiment are illustrated on pages 140 and 141. In this early stage, we averaged the EEG data across all frequencies to represent the intensity of brain activity, with red indicating higher levels of brain activation. At this time, we did not record assessment responses and brain activity simultaneously. Instead, participants completed the ACI assessment as they normally would, and then, within a 72-hour period, we showed them the 18 items again in a random order to record their brain activity.

We used standardized low-resolution brain electromagnetic tomography (sLORETA) for analyzing and visualizing the voxel images of the participants' brain activity in real time. These images depicted the average brain activity in the left hemisphere for each ACI item, marking our first steps in visualizing the decision-making process in the brain. Initially, we had not yet explored the significance of analyzing different regions of the brain or the variations in brain activation frequencies.

The findings from this first experiment were both immediate and thrilling. Even a cursory examination of the results revealed that the items at both extremes of internal and external rankings showed significantly more intense activity (indicated by red areas) than the items in the middle. This discovery was a breakthrough, opening up new avenues for our research into various aspects of brain function:

- Prefrontal lobe asymmetry
- The role of gamma activity in emotional responses
- Identification of precognitive events
- The connection to event-related potentials
- The study of neural networks and connectivity

THE FIVE SCIENCES OF SELF

CLIENT EXTERNAL ASSESSMENT RESPONSE ORDERING MATCHED TO REAL TIME BRAIN ACTIVITY

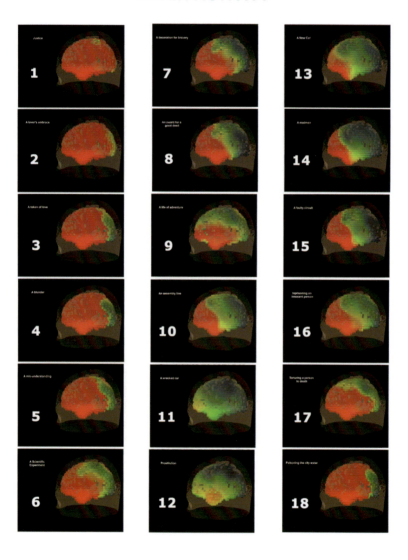

These initial brain images (pages 140 and 141) show increased brain activation for items on each end of this "like versus dislike" continuum.

THE SCIENCE OF THE HARTMAN VALUE PROFILE

CLIENT INTERNAL ASSESSMENT RESPONSE ORDERING MATCHED TO REAL TIME BRAIN ACTIVITY

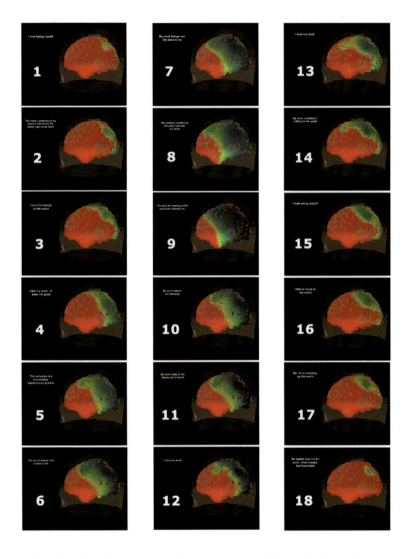

This initial study suggested that the extent of like or dislike could be matched to brain activity as seen in these images (pages 140 and 141).

HVP IN THE FUTURE

The author who wrote, *Freedom to Live: The Robert Hartman Story* said it best:

> "Robert Hartman's legacy to us in formal axiology is a response to the experiences of his own life. Within this theory lies the foundation for a science of value, but as he noted, it is only the beginning. The theory needs clarification, amplification, and enhancement. Continuing Hartman's work is the task for those with the vision to 'organize the good' in the world."
>
> —Arthur R. Ellis

We at TTI Success Insights plan to be contributors to this challenging and fulfilling work.

WHAT YOU SHOULD KNOW ABOUT THE HARTMAN VALUE PROFILE
by Carissa

The Hartman Value Profile is a tool designed to clarify how you perceive yourself in contrast to your view of the world. It aims to illuminate your personal niche within both your immediate surroundings and the broader context of life. The Acumen Capacity Index (ACI), drawing from the Hartman Value Profile, is instrumental in helping you discover your purpose or place. It's a robust assessment instrument that evaluates how clearly you understand yourself and the world around you, pinpointing the blind spots that emotional biases may create.

CONCLUSION

SCIENCES OF SELF IN BUSINESS TODAY AND TOMORROW

THE FUTURE IS NOW!

Success in business and our daily lives is directly tied to our ability to be self-aware and make necessary adjustments to our brain-body alignment. Each of the TTI Success Insights' sciences helps us become more aware of who we are and how we operate as human beings. But awareness is not enough. The goal is to transform—to take this valuable information and make adjustments to our lived experiences. And that transformation comes from many sparks throughout our lives, not just one spark in time. The process is a journey, not a destination.

Consider someone at work, in your family, or even someone in your community, who likes to proclaim a statement like, "This is who I am. You can take it or leave it," when faced with an interpersonal conflict. This person is not committed to change, reflection, or examining how their behavior impacts others around them. If they were to take the first step in learning about themselves using any of the five sciences, they could technically begin to achieve self-awareness. They would be able to label themselves with descriptors from the assessments and may even be proud of their behavior when it works to their advantage. They may become more self-aware, but they are not on a transformational journey.

> **In the words of Bill Bonnstetter, "Our tools provide insights into self, not excuses for one's behaviors."**

The transformation occurs when this person learns how their behavior impacts others and begins to act on it—when self-awareness becomes self-regulation. They may realize they are quick to judge when someone else is speaking, therefore instead of replying with their own opinions to prove a point, they decide to ask questions that help further the conversation. They might discover their innate need for quick information is causing conflict with team members who are driven by making a safe and well-researched decision, so they establish deadlines that everyone can agree on together. They may learn they can be perceived as detached or apathetic when they are under stress, so they practice one minute of mindful breathing before entering the boardroom to calm their internal thought pattern. These are all small examples of transformation, but even the most minuscule of adjustments can drive impactful change, especially when the practice becomes a habit.

Better yet, the transformative potential of using these sciences is exceedingly practical. TTI Success Insights is not fabricating outlandish methods for behavioral change that seem unachievable. We are simply helping people to discover the ways in which they show up in the world. Once you can name your behavioral style, understand what motivates you, or identify the skills you are best at, you can begin to uniquely contribute value in all areas of life—whether it's at home, in the workplace, or with friends. More importantly, you can learn how to integrate your style and skills with the diverse

CONCLUSION

individuals around you, achieving a synergy that may have otherwise been left unfulfilled.

The small changes you can implement in your life can lead to big wins. For example, after taking an assessment, you may learn that abrupt change in your day causes stress because you like to live your life at a steady and predictable pace. At work, you might alert your supervisor that you'd prefer to be notified of any change as early as possible to give you time to adjust. At home, you may decide to hold weekly family meetings to get everyone's events and obligations on the calendar—helping to eliminate any surprises. Of course, unplanned happenings are inevitable and the ability to be flexible is key, but simply knowing this about yourself can help you navigate life differently and aid in understanding your adverse reactions when things happen outside of your control.

When it comes to workplace effectiveness, healthy, dynamic, high-functioning teams are working on two things at once: the business tasks at hand and the orchestration of the humanistic elements of their team. Big-picture people take on the visionary aspects of the project, and those who are more detail-oriented contribute to the areas that need fine-tuning. Individuals who prefer to work in the background are given tasks to help connect the dots, while those who prefer being a spokesperson are asked to publicly present project findings. It all comes down to leveraging the strengths, skill sets, and preferences of individuals on the team.

There is no doubt the five sciences of self can improve an individual's performance in the workplace by identifying these exact characteristics. How many articles do we read while attempting to unpack the mysteries of what motivates a team? How to improve company culture? How to effectively achieve goals? The insights required may not be immediately apparent but can often be found within the five sciences of self. Exploring the assessments offered by TTI can help identify personal attributes that have remained unrecognized. Recognizing these aspects can play a crucial role in improving team dynamics and progress.

Our lived life and our workplace culture are complex and require a multitude of tools to uncover and address the intricate issues of behavioral interactions, differing values and motivators, and all of the personal and professional stressors that clients encounter daily. To go one step further than simply identifying a company's assessment needs, TTI is on the cusp of offering organization-wide data analytics and grouped psychometrics that will allow people to compare and contrast different teams and sub-groupings within their organization at a glance. Analyzing vast amounts of data will help identify patterns and correlations, thus providing a deeper understanding of individual and team capabilities. TTI is positioned to help our users identify the correct combination of assessment tools and train them to maximize their application.

With the goal of transformation in mind, the future of TTI's personal assessments for professional development and hiring is likely to involve a combination of traditional methods and innovative technologies to enhance accuracy, objectivity, and efficiency. Technological advances coincide exceptionally well with self-report assessments and our continued research on the brain regarding decision-making and mental well-being.

Imagine . . .

Imagine a future where, along with your regular morning routines of getting ready for work, you have another quick readiness check.

CONCLUSION

You place a small wireless headband on, and your computer or phone screen lights up with a status report on your "emotional fitness." The computerized voice quickly runs through its routine and, in 15 seconds, delivers an update:

> "Prefrontal cortex asymmetry within acceptable levels. If time allows, it is recommended you arrange for 30 minutes of mindset management activities to lower gamma output in the right prefrontal cortex and increase alpha symmetry. Have a nice day."

Our current and continued neurological advancements, along with the evolution of AI and machine learning, will augment our assessments and create integration into our daily lives that could be as ubiquitous as wearing a pair of glasses or carrying a cell phone. This will open the door to continuous feedback loops, resulting in behavioral modification and ultimately, greater personal and professional growth and development.

We are already very accustomed, if not borderline addicted, to tracking components of our physical health with apps, smartwatches, and other devices. The societal surge in tracking one's daily movement, heart rate, and caloric burn has become increasingly prevalent in the past several years, to the point where we rely on our devices to tell us to move after we have been sitting too long.

In contrast, we have not focused on data that drives our behavioral health with nearly the same vigor. We have apps that help us focus on our mindfulness and meditation practices, but we are missing the science-based measurement of our own neurological progress. There has not been an easy way to see our brain changing once we establish a mindful habit—we just have to trust it. Without measurement, we cannot methodically improve, just as one cannot expect to achieve better physical fitness if they do not track their workouts. Consider a world in which we are equally as dedicated to measuring, and therefore modifying, our behaviors, reactions, and emotions as we are to our daily step count. We can focus on overall well-being in a way we haven't before by scaling our current research and integrating mindset management tools into an easy-access platform for people to use in their daily routines.

There is also the potential to evolve our actions and reactions into gamified simulations that allow individuals to practice and demonstrate their skills in a more engaging and realistic environment. This approach will allow the user to refine their interactions in a socially safe environment, thus leading once again to personal and professional development.

REAL SCIENCE: THE FIVE SCIENCES OF SELF

TTI continues to meet the challenges such as ensuring the validity and reliability of self-report assessments, maintaining candidate privacy, and addressing potential biases in algorithms and data interpretation. These will continue to be areas of focus and improvement in the future.

The most affirming element of these sciences is that they are, in fact, true sciences backed by extensive traditional quantitative analysis as well as cutting-edge neurological decision-making response processing. EEG imaging conducted in our research allows us to see brain activity in real-time when someone is faced with positive or negative stimuli. Not only does this help us validate our self-report assessments, ensuring the assessment questions elicit clear responses in alignment with one's thoughts, but they also allow us to see how the brain is processing data before the mind can register a conscious thought. It is rare for someone to have the opportunity to measure one's own neurological improvement in "soft skills." Typically, we

CONCLUSION

simply have to trust our intuition that we are improving when we commit to working on our behaviors, emotions, and reactions. It's not the same as deciding to lift weights and eventually seeing muscle growth over time, but TTI has validated that you can train your brain just like any other muscle in the body. As we tie neurological research to self-improvement, TTI continues the quest to understand the ways in which people make decisions, define their skill sets, and respond to positive and negative stimuli.

> **The impact of the five sciences of self has boundless possibilities.**

Think of all the layers of interactions you have in just one day. You interact with family members, coworkers, friends, strangers, and even with your own brain inside your thoughts and self-talk. Each of us experiences thousands of interactions over the course of one day, and choosing to embark on a journey of self-awareness has the potential to impact every single one of those interactions. And the best part is, the first steps of the journey are small—just one drop in the pond.

Start with self-reflection. Seek to understand why you do what you do. The next time you react to something, take a moment to reflect and ask yourself what prompted you to respond that way. Ask yourself what you want at this stage of your life and what you can do to move in the right direction. No matter if you want to improve your relationships with others, get promoted to your dream job, or achieve a goal with your team, the starting place is almost always within you.

These sciences have the potential to unlock undiscovered traits that could be holding you back in the workplace or at home. With focused effort and a little help from the five sciences of self, you can begin to discover, utilize, and enhance your skills to work to your advantage.

The journey to self-awareness has no end. There is no way to arrive at a so-called self-improvement finish line, but the journey is the destination. All you need to do is start.

CONNECT

To learn more about how you can use brain imaging to gain personal insights or to connect with Dr. Ronald Bonnstetter or Carissa Gwerder Collazo:

Email: info@mindsciencecenter.com
MindScienceCenter.com
ttisi.com

ACKNOWLEDGMENTS

DR. RON BONNSTETTER

As I reflect on this project, I am in awe of all the past thought leaders mentioned in this book who have laid a solid foundation for building our past and future. We truly stand on the shoulders of giants. From this firm foundation, Bill and his son David Bonnstetter were able to take these grounding concepts to new heights. Their vision has continued to be expanded by many key contributors, including Dr. Eric Gehrig, who envisioned our extensive technical reports, and Dustin Hebets, who helped connect decision-making with real-time brain imaging.

I also want to thank my wife, Nicolette, and our family, as well as the TTI family, who lent their support, encouragement, and ideas.

This most recent stepping stone in the process of understanding self would only have occurred with the vision of Ron Price, TTI President, and the almost daily encouragement of the Aloha Publishing team, especially Heather Goetter and Maryanna Young.

Lastly, I am grateful for my co-author, Carissa, who was willing to join this journey of documenting our evolving saga and who stands ready to take this emerging field to the next level.

My dream is that we will look back and smile at how this point in time has continued to evolve as humanity probes deeper into the sciences of self. My hope is that this journey will transform self-awareness and result in yet-to-be-discovered personal fulfillment. Enjoy the journey.

CARISSA GWERDER COLLAZO, MS

I'd first like to thank my husband, Fito, for listening to me read sections of this book aloud over and over as I worked through my writing process and for absorbing all of my nervous excitement as we completed each stage of the manuscript. You provide me with the balance and strength I need in my life.

I would also like to thank my parents, Paul and Judy, for supporting me in every way imaginable from childhood to adulthood and being my number one fans in every endeavor I have ever pursued. I would not be in this position without you.

A special shout-out to my siblings, Jeremy, Caleb, and Aleea, for doubling as some of my best friends and being willing to listen when I need encouragement, both in this process and otherwise.

Of course, I would also like to thank Dr. Ron Bonnstetter for including me in this project and providing me with the opportunity to carve a space for myself in this industry. I am exceedingly grateful for his guidance and empowerment every single day.

I'd like to express appreciation for Ron Price and David Bonnstetter for their exceptional leadership and vision in steering the company's direction, for their inclusiveness in making me a part of this remarkable journey, and for Dustin Hebets and Rick McPartlin for their overall support and reassurance throughout my time at TTI.

Finally, I want to express deep gratitude to Aloha Publishing, the epitome of professionalism and excellence. Their passion and thoroughness truly allowed our stories to come to life, and Heather Goetter and Maryanna Young's expertise and belief in us have been nothing short of miraculous. Collaborating with them has been a remarkable opportunity, and I am eternally grateful for their guidance during this experience.

ABOUT THE AUTHORS

Dr. Ronald J. Bonnstetter is a distinguished figure in the realm of behavioral research and educational methodologies, actively contributing to the field through his groundbreaking work with brain imaging at TTI Success Insights. His unique blend of expertise in psychology, education, and technology positions him at the forefront of applying scientific insights to real-world challenges in education and corporate environments.

Currently, Dr. Bonnstetter serves in a pivotal role at TTI Success Insights, where his innovative approach to behavioral assessment is revolutionizing the way individuals and organizations approach personal and professional development. Through his leadership, the company has pioneered the use of advanced brain imaging techniques to enhance the accuracy and impact of its assessment tools. These tools are designed to offer deep insights into individual behavioral styles, motivators, and competencies, enabling more effective communication, leadership strategies, and team dynamics.

Dr. Bonnstetter's influence extends far beyond the development of assessment tools; he is a visionary dedicated to bridging the gap between cutting-edge research and everyday application. His efforts aim to empower individuals and organizations to unlock their full potential by gaining a deeper understanding of the brain's role in behavior and interaction. Through his work, Dr. Bonnstetter continues to inspire a wide audience, championing the use of scientific discovery to enhance human potential and create environments where people can excel.

ABOUT THE AUTHORS

Carissa Gwerder Collazo, MS is a dynamic force at the intersection of neuroscience and organizational behavior, bringing fresh perspectives and innovative methodologies to the study of workplace dynamics and personal development. Her expertise in cognitive science and her commitment to applying neuroscientific principles to improve organizational outcomes have made her a vital asset to the team at TTI Success Insights. Carissa's work primarily revolves around leveraging cutting-edge neuroscience research to enhance understanding of decision-making processes, emotional intelligence, and team cohesion within professional settings.

Carissa's passion for exploring the brain's influence on behavior and her dedication to using this knowledge to foster healthier, more productive workplace environments are evident in her contributions to the field.

Beyond her contributions to research and development, Carissa is a mentor and advocate for the application of neuroscience in everyday organizational practices. Her vision encompasses a future where the integration of brain science in business strategies is standard, enhancing the well-being and performance of individuals and teams alike. Through her ongoing work at TTI Success Insights, she continues to inspire and influence the realms of neuroscience and organizational development.

Carissa currently lives in Arizona with her husband. When not performing EEG brain scans, she loves to escape to the mountains for hiking adventures and bake cookies to make up for the lost calories.

INDEX

Activity Vector Analysis (AVA), 40–43
Acumen Capacity Index (ACI), 120–123, 128, 131, 138–139, 143
Air Force, 41
Alcoa Aluminum, 127
Allport, Gordon, 69, 71, 127
Allport and Vernon Study of Values (SOV), 69–70
Allport-Vernon-Lindzey Study of Value (SOV), 70–71
American Psychological Association (APA), 29–31
APA Handbook of Testing and Assessment in Psychology, 30
Aristotle, 7, 58–60, 62
artificial intelligence (AI), 74, 83, 94–95, 115–116, 149
assessments
    Acumen Capacity Index assessment, 120–123, 128, 131, 138–139, 143
    behavioral assessment, 7, 12, 15, 18–21, 25, 29, 33–52, 81–82, 145–151
    benefits of, 15–16, 19–20
    client external assessment, 140
    client internal assessment, 141
    DISC assessment, 33–52
    emotional assessment, 97–118
    Hartman Value Profile assessment, 119–143
    motivation assessment, 54–74
    personal assessment, 11–12, 15–16, 47–49, 62, 81–82, 106, 148
    personality assessment, 15–16, 18, 25, 27, 44–45, 49–51, 68–71, 129
    psychological assessment, 23–24, 29–31, 42–43, 67–69, 119–143
    self-assessment, 7–12, 15–16, 52
    self-report assessment, 8–9, 93, 148–151
    tools for, 7–12, 15–16

value assessment, 119–143
　　workplace competency assessment, 77–96
Attitude Index, 131
attitudes, 33, 39, 68–72, 86, 110, 131
axiology, 8, 119–121, 123–138, 142

Bar-On, Reuven, 104–105, 108
Bar-On model, 104–106
behavioral assessment, 7, 12, 15, 18–21, 25, 29, 33–52, 81–82, 145–151
Behavioral Continuum, 34–35
behavioral factors, 33–39
behavioral styles, 12–13, 17–24, 33–52, 116, 146–150
Bonnstetter, Bill J., 11–12, 17–22, 32, 46–48, 70–71, 87–89, 146
Bonnstetter, David, 21, 46–48
Bonnstetter, Dr. Ronald, 10–11, 153
brain imaging, 8–9, 16, 22–27, 30, 49–51, 73, 93, 138–141, 150
business skills, 88–89. *See also* workplace competencies
Business Values Inventory, 70

capabilities, 7–9, 64, 83, 105, 117, 148. *See also* skills
Carlson Marketing Group, 45–46
Carnegie Foundation for the Advancement of Teaching, 82–83
Clarke, Walter, 40–43
Cleaver, John "Clipper," 43–45
client external assessment, 140
client internal assessment, 141
cognitive intelligence (IQ), 98, 102, 106–108
cognitive skills, 81, 85–86, 92
Collazo, Carissa Gwerder, 25–26, 52, 75, 96, 118, 143, 153
Columbia University, 39, 65
Complete Leader Program, 99
Council of Profit Sharing Industries, 127
COVID-19 pandemic, 113–114
Critical Examination of the Construct Validity of the TTI Performance DNA Survey for the Purpose of Differentiating the

INDEX

Entrepreneurially-Minded Engineer, 79

Darwin, Charles, 60
Davis, John, 130
Descartes, René, 60
Dietrich, Sandra L., 79–80
DISC
    application of, 34–52
    assessments, 33–52
    behavioral factors, 33–39
    behavioral styles, 33–52
    compliance dimension, 33–39
    concept of, 33–36
    dimensions of, 33–39
    dominance dimension, 33–39
    explanation of, 7, 12–13, 33–36
    future of, 49–51
    history of, 37–38
    influence dimension, 33–39
    job performance, 40–42
    leadership roles, 41–47
    models, 37–47
    origin of, 16
    power of, 37
    science of, 33–52
    steadiness dimension, 33–39
    Style Insights DISC wheel, 12–13
    success and, 33–52
    theories, 21–23, 38–44
    traits, 33–42
DISC model, 37–47
DISC theory, 21–23, 38–44
DISC traits, 33–42
DISC wheel, 12–13
disciplines
    DISC, 7–8, 12–13, 16, 33–52

emotional intelligence, 7–8, 16, 97–118
Hartman Value Profile, 7–8, 16, 119–143
motivation, 7–8, 16, 53–75
workplace competencies, 7–8, 16, 77–96
see also five sciences
Disney, Walt, 124
DNA 23, 85, 87–90, 92
DNA 25, 92
DNA Job Report, 77, 91
DNA surveys, 77–80
DNA Talent Report, 77, 91
DNA workplace competencies, 77–80, 85–94

"Education for Life and Work: Developing Transferable Knowledge and Skills in the 21st Century," 85
electroencephalogram (EEG), 23–24, 30, 49–51, 138–141, 150. *See also* brain imaging
Ellis, Arthur R., 142
emotional assessment, 97–118
Emotional Intelligence, 108–109
emotional intelligence/emotional quotient (EI/EQ)
  adaptability, 97–98, 106, 111
  application of, 104–118
  assessments, 97–118
  COVID-19 pandemic and, 113–114
  current assessments, 110–115
  empathy, 97, 102–106, 109–111, 114–116
  explanation of, 8, 97–98
  future of, 114–117
  history of, 100–101
  intelligence quotient and, 98, 102, 106–108
  internal motivation, 109, 111
  interpersonal skills, 102, 106
  intrapersonal skills, 105
  key components of, 105–111
  leadership roles, 98–99, 109, 112–115

INDEX

models of, 104–110, 116–117
mood and, 100, 106
motivation and, 109, 111
origin of, 16
relationship management, 97–118
research on, 98–117
science of, 97–118
self-awareness, 97–118
self-expression, 105
self-management, 97–118
self-regulation, 100, 107–118
skill sets, 8, 97–118
social awareness, 97, 111
social intelligence, 101–102, 107
social regulation, 111
social skills, 8, 104–105, 109, 116
stress management, 98, 104–106, 111, 113–114
success and, 97–118
of today, 110–115
transformative effects of, 98–99
understanding, 98–118
Emotional Quotient Inventory (EQ-i), 104–106
Emotional Quotient Talent Report, 101, 110–112
emotional skills, 97–118
empowerment, 7–9, 48, 54–55
engineering management executive (EME), 80
extrinsic dimension, 8, 119–120, 127, 132–137
extrinsic motivation, 54, 64, 72
extrinsic value, 8, 127, 132–137

five sciences
    DISC, 7–8, 12–13, 16, 33–52
    emotional intelligence, 7–8, 16, 97–118
    future of, 145–152
    Hartman Value Profile, 7–8, 16, 119–143
    motivation, 7–8, 16, 53–75
    workplace competencies, 7–8, 16, 77–96

Four Branch Model of Emotional Intelligence, 107
Frankel, Viktor, 127–128
Freedom to Live: The Robert Hartman Story, 123–124, 142
Freud, Sigmund, 62
Fromm, Eric, 128

Galileo, 128
Geier, John G., 45–46
Glaucon, 125
goals, achieving, 53–75, 80–89, 111, 123, 147–151
goals, setting, 53–75, 80
Goleman, Daniel, 8, 99, 108–110, 117
"goodness" concept, 58–59, 124–129, 132–136, 142

Hall, Kathryn, 61
Hartman, Rita Emanuel, 124–125
Hartman, Robert S., 8, 119, 123–134, 138, 142
Hartman Institute, 130, 132
Hartman Value Profile (HVP)
    Acumen Capacity Index and, 120–123, 128, 131, 138–139, 143
    application of, 120–143
    assessments, 119–143
    axiology and, 8, 119–121, 123–138, 142
    biases and, 120–121, 131–135, 143
    brain imaging and, 138–141
    dimensions of, 8, 119–121, 127, 131–138
    explanation of, 8, 119–123, 127–130
    extrinsic dimension, 8, 119–120, 127, 132–137
    in future, 142
    "goodness" concept and, 124–129, 132–136, 142
    history of, 123–129
    intrinsic dimension, 8, 119–120, 127, 132–137
    leadership roles, 121–122, 130
    origin of, 16
    research on, 127–139

rules of axiology and, 132–138
science of, 119–143
self views and, 120–121, 129–131, 136, 143
success and, 119–143
systemic dimension, 8, 119–120, 127, 132–137
of today, 131–132, 138–139
understanding, 119–143
valuation process, 119–143
value judgments, 119–121, 128–131, 136–138
worldviews and, 120–121, 129–131, 136, 143
Harvard University, 61, 83, 108
Hebrew University, 65–66
Herzberg, Frederick, 64
Hierarchy of Needs, 64
Hierarchy of Value, 128–129, 134
Hitler, Adolf, 124
Hull, Clark, 62
Husserl, Edmund, 127

intelligence quotient (IQ), 98, 102, 106–108
internal motivation, 109, 111
interpersonal skills, 81, 84–88, 92–93, 102, 106, 121
intrapersonal skills, 85, 87, 92, 105
intrinsic dimension, 8, 119–120, 127, 132–137
intrinsic motivation, 47, 54, 64, 68, 72, 75
intrinsic value, 8, 127, 132–137
Iowa State Teachers College, 46

James, William, 60–61
job performance, 21, 27–28, 40–42, 77–91, 113, 147–148

Klassen, Peter T., 71

leadership
DISC and, 41–47
emotional intelligence and, 98–99, 109, 112–115

Hartman Value Profile and, 121–122, 130
motivation and, 54, 72–74
workplace competencies and, 77–89
Lecky, Prescott, 7, 33, 39–40, 43
Likert scale, 31
Lindzey, Gardner, 69–71
Lion, Angie, 98–99

Man's Search For Meaning, 128
Manual of Interpretation, 131
Marston, William Moulton, 7, 33, 38–40, 43
Maslow, Abraham, 64, 127–129
Maslow's Hierarchy of Needs, 64
Maslow's Hierarchy of Value, 128–129, 134
Mathematical Principles of Natural Philosophy, 125
Mayer, John D., 8, 106–108, 117
Mayer-Salovey Model, 107–108
McClelland, David, 64, 108
McDougall, William, 61
Mefford, David, 130–131, 137
Mefford, Vera, 130–131
MIT, 84, 127
Moore, George E., 125–126
motivation
    12 Driving Forces, 54–56, 72
    academic performance and, 55–57
    achievement motivation theory, 64
    application of, 55–75
    arousal theory, 63
    assessments, 54–74
    categories of, 54–55
    drive theory, 62–63
    driving forces, 53–63, 72
    emotional intelligence and, 109, 111
    equity theory, 65
    expectancy theory, 64

INDEX

    explanation of, 7, 53–57
    extrinsic motivation, 54, 64, 72
    in future, 73–74
    goals and, 53–75
    goal-setting theory, 64
    grand theories of, 59–63
    hierarchy of needs, 64
    history of, 57–59
    incentive theory, 63
    incentives and, 53–54, 62–63
    instinct theory, 60–62
    internal motivation, 109, 111
    intrinsic motivation, 47, 54, 64, 68, 72, 75
    leadership roles, 54, 72–74
    mini-theories of, 63–65
    opponent-process theory, 65
    origin of, 16
    rewards and, 63–64
    science of, 53–75
    self-determination theory, 64
    self-efficacy theory, 64
    success and, 53–75
    surgical training and, 55–57
    theoretical motivation, 54–66
    theories of, 54–71
    theory of will, 60
    three needs theory, 64
    of today, 72–73
    two-factory theory, 64
    understanding, 53–75
    values and, 65–71
Motivation Insights, 71–72
Mowrer, O. Hobart, 102–103

National Research Council (NRC), 85, 92
National Science Foundation, 55

Nationwide Insurance, 127
natural science, 14–15
Nature of Human Values, The, 71
New York Times, 108
Newton, Sir Isaac, 125
Nicomachean Ethics, 59
Northwestern University, 125

Ohio State University, 127

Pattern and Growth in Personality, 71
Payne, Wayne, 104–105
Performax Systems International, Inc., 45
personal assessment, 11–12, 15–16, 47–49, 62, 81–82, 106, 148
Personal Interests, Attitudes, and Values (PIAV), 70–72
Personal Motivation and Engagement Legacy (PME), 72
Personal Profile System, 46
personal skills, 77–82, 87–92
Personal Talents, Skills, and Insights Report (PTSI), 131
personality assessment, 15–16, 18, 25, 27, 44–45, 49–51, 68–71, 129
personality traits, 25, 27, 44–45, 49–53
personality types, 68–71
Phenomenology of Man as a Valuing Subject, 137
Plato, 7, 58–59, 125
Price, Ron, 100, 120–121
Principia Ethica, 125
psychological assessment, 23–24, 29–31, 42–43, 67–69, 119–143
psychological theories, 23–24, 33, 38–43, 62
psychometric analysis, 27, 31, 81, 129, 148
psychometric scale, 31

relationship management, 97–118
Republic, The, 58, 125
Richter Scale, 136
Rokeach, Milton, 71
Ross School of Business, 84

INDEX

Sagan, Carl, 13
Salovey, Peter, 8, 106–108, 117
Schwartz, Shalom H., 65–68
Schwartz Theory of Basic Human Values, 66–68
Science of Self, 19, 22–24, 32, 75
Sears Roebuck & Company, 127
self-assessment, 7–12, 15–16, 52
self-awareness, 8–10, 15, 36, 58, 87, 97–118, 120–121, 145–146, 151–152
self-determination, 64
self-efficacy, 64
self-expression, 105
self-management, 80, 83–85, 97–118
self-reflection, 79, 151
self-regulation, 8, 39, 87, 100, 107–118, 146
self-report assessment, 8–9, 93, 148–151
self-views, 120–121, 129–131, 136, 143
Shero, Dr. Laura, 113–114
Shirokauer, Robert, 123
Siebert Institute, 130
Siemens, 130
skills
    business skills, 88–89
    cognitive skills, 81, 85–86, 92
    emotional skills, 97–118
    interpersonal skills, 81, 84–88, 92–93, 102, 106, 121
    intrapersonal skills, 85, 87, 92, 105
    personal skills, 77–82, 87–92
    skill sets, 8, 47, 77–95, 97–118, 147–151
    social skills, 8, 104–105, 109, 116
    soft skills, 77–95, 150
Sloan School of Management, 84
Sluyter, D. J., 107
social awareness, 97, 111
social intelligence, 101–102, 107
social regulation, 111

social sciences, 7–8, 14–16, 65, 85, 128–130, 137
social skills, 8, 104–105, 109, 116
Socrates, 7, 58, 125
soft skills, 77–95, 150
Spranger, Eduard, 54, 68–72
standardized low-resolution brain electromagnetic tomography (sLORETA), 30, 139
Stanford Research Institute (SRI) International, 82–83
stress management, 98, 104–106, 111, 113–114, 146–147
Study of Emotion: Developing Emotional Intelligence, 104
Study of Values, A, 71
Study of Values (SOV), 69–71
Style Insights DISC wheel, 12–13
Style Insights format, 34
Style Insights Technical Manual Version 1.0, 37
success
    DISC and, 33–52
    emotional intelligence and, 97–118
    five sciences and, 7–75, 77–143, 145–152
    Hartman Value Profile and, 119–143
    motivation and, 53–75
    workplace competencies and, 77–96
surgical training study, 55–57
systemic dimension, 8, 119–120, 127, 132–137
systemic value, 8, 127, 132–137

Target Training International, Ltd., 47
team building, 21, 28, 37–47, 72–74, 89, 115
team capabilities, 83, 148
team cohesion, 41, 45, 75, 118
team dynamics, 16, 27–28, 37–52, 72–92, 98, 146–151
teamwork, 81–88, 92
Tesla, 134
Theory of Basic Human Values, 66–68
Thorndike, Edward Lee, 101–102
Treatise of Man, 60

INDEX

TriMetrix (TTI) System, 56
TTI Performance DNA Survey, 79–80
TTI Success Insights
    axiology and, 8, 119–121, 123–138, 142
    DISC and, 34–51
    emotional intelligence and, 97–118
    five sciences of, 7–9, 15–75, 77–143, 145–152
    founding of, 47
    Hartman Value Profile and, 120–142
    history of, 20–22
    motivation and, 54–74
    research and, 9, 16, 19–29, 32, 145–151
    results of, 27–28
    scientific proof behind, 22–24
    workplace competencies and, 77–95
TTI Success Insights Emotional Quotient 2019 Technical Manual Version 1.2, 101
TTI Success Insights Emotional Quotient report, 101, 110–112
TTI Success Insights Motivation Insights Technical Manual Version 1.0, 71
TTI Success Insights Style Insights Technical Manual Version 1.0, 37
Types of Men, 68

Universal Language DISC, 34
University of Cambridge, 84
University of Heidelberg, 130
University of Michigan, 65, 84
University of Nebraska, 13
University of Northern Iowa, 46
University of Tennessee, 127, 130, 132
University of Wisconsin–Madison, 65

value
    assessments, 119–143
    axiology and, 8, 119–121, 123–138, 142
    biases and, 120–121, 131–135, 143

defining, 132–138
  dimensions of, 8, 119–121, 127, 131–138
  extrinsic value, 8, 127, 132–137
  hierarchy of, 128–129, 134
  intrinsic value, 8, 127, 132–137
  rules of axiology and, 132–138
  study of, 127–131
  systemic value, 8, 127, 132–137
  valuation process, 119–138
  value judgments, 119–121, 128–131, 136–138
  see also Hartman Value Profile
values
  basic human values, 66–71
  model of, 67
  motivation and, 65–71
  research on, 65–70
  role of, 65–67
  study of, 69–71
  theory of, 66–71
  types of, 66–71
Vernon, Philip E., 69
Volkswagen, 130

Watson, Russel J., 70–71
Wonder Woman, 38–39
Woodworth, Robert S., 62
Working with Emotional Intelligence, 108
workplace competencies
  360-degree feedback surveys, 81, 91–93
  application of, 85–95
  assessments, 77–96
  business skills, 88–89
  cognitive skills, 81, 85–86, 92
  defining, 85–87, 90–94
  DNA competencies, 77–80, 85–94
  DNA surveys, 77–80

educational strategies, 79, 82–89, 93–95
explanation of, 8, 77–79
future of, 94–95
history of, 81–82
interpersonal skills, 81, 84–88, 92–93
interview questions, 90–91
intrapersonal skills, 85, 87, 92
job performance, 77–91
key competencies, 87–90
leadership roles, 77–89
origin of, 16
personal skills, 77–82, 87–92
science of, 77–96
soft skills, 77–95, 150
success and, 77–96
team dynamics, 77–92
teamwork, 81–88, 92
theories of, 84–85, 90–95
of today, 94
understanding, 77–96
workplace standards, 84–87, 95
worldviews, 120–121, 129–131, 136, 143
Wright, Frank Lloyd, 133

Yale University, 127

Zucker, Gerhard, 124